Being Afrikan

Rediscovering the Traditional Unhu-Ubuntu-Botho Pathways
of Being Human

Mandivamba Rukuni

mandala publishers

ISBN 978-0-620-39480-2

Edited by Reinhild M Niebuhr

Cover design and lay-out by Reinhild M Niebuhr
Printed and bound by Business Print, Meiring Naudé Road, Brummeria, Pretoria, South Africa

This book is dedicated to my parents, my family, my Rozvi clan, and a special dedication goes to the Afrikan ancestors, whose wisdom we now desperately need, in order to rebuild our beloved motherland, Afrika.

Being Afrikan

Mandivamba Rukuni

mandala publishers

ACKNOWLEDGEMENTS

There are numerous people from my youth to today who helped shape me, and therefore shape this indigenous knowledge into a coherent set of ideas. I am grateful to all of you and of course you are too numerous to remember and/or mention all by name. I am grateful to Reinhild Niebuhr for her encouragement and belief in the book, and then editing the manuscript.

Mandivamba Rukuni

AFFILIATION AND DISCLAIMER

Professor Mandivamba Rukuni is currently the Regional Director of the W.K. Kellogg Foundation Afrika programme, and before that he was a Professor of Agricultural Economics with the University of Zimbabwe. All ideas and content in this book are, however, attributable to the author in his personal capacity and do not necessarily reflect those of the organizations the author has been affiliated with.

FOREWORD

Professor Mandivamba Rukuni's book *Being Afrikan* represents a major wake-up call to Afrikans, to retrieve their collective cultural memory and use this as a way forward to development and modernity. I have yet to come across another book, which so succinctly, lucidly and without any linguistic frills or verbosity, sets out and achieves a credible diagnosis and resounding analysis of the Afrikan crisis.

The ideas expressed here are, however, not simply a diagnostic analysis. They go far beyond this, and offer solutions and answers to the problems we face as Afrikans.

Indeed, the appearance of this book leaves no doubt in my mind that, in as far as the idea of an *Afrikan Renaissance* is concerned, we are seeing light at the cnd of a long tunnel. The message of Mandivamba Rukuni is that we must go back to our roots, salvage what is wholesome and best in this, and use it as the basis for our way forward. It is very much in the spirit of the Afrikan idea of *Sankofa (Sankofa* is an Akan word which means, "we must go back and reclaim our past so that we can move forward; so that we understand why and how we came to be who we are today.") .

The book which is philosophically anchored in the notion of *Unhu-Ubuntu-Botho* recognizes the universal and humanistic qualities of this spirit and ethos. It embraces humanity as a whole, whilst locating this embrace on the foundations of an enlightened Afrikanism, which celebrates all, while not diminishing its Afrikan mainsprings.

The appearance of this text is timely because it comes at a juncture in history, when Afrikans are dogged by gnawing despair and persistent self-doubt. The Rozvi spirits are speaking through Rukuni and their message is loud and clear.

This book will become, in time, recognized as a clarion call to Afrikanism in the tradition of the best of its kind, in our times. I see it as an initial shot of a cultural movement (*Sankofa Movement*) of Afrikans towards advancement and modernity.

Kwesi Kwaa Prah
Cape Town
September 2007

Table of Contents

Introduction

My voice is not the only one: unless we Afrikans rediscover ourselves, our roots and heritage, and embrace and understand, even love everything that made our ancestors survive and thrive for millions of years, unless we understand how our ancestors succeeded so well in creating a dynamic society in the past, we cannot create a new, modern Afrikan society.

Afrika is the place where ape-like creatures evolved into humans. This transformation is and was the process of becoming human. So when Shona people or Bantu people say *Unhu* or *Ubuntu* or *Botho*– meaning 'being' or 'being human' – it means that our ancestors knew right from the beginning that the change from animal to the 'awareness of being' is really the process of achieving a higher level of consciousness.

This higher level of consciousness made that our ancestors recognised that you cannot be a human being without other human beings around you. Genetically, we are still animals. God evolved us from a type of animal. This means that we are part of the animal kingdom, we are strongly connected to nature. The only difference is that we have been blessed by God as a species because he made it possible for us to relate to one another in a more meaningful way. This means that you are only there because of others. Without someone else seeing you or relating to you, you cannot really be human. Animals will see you simply as another type of animal: you are either an enemy or a prey. Just think how a lion in the wild sees you!

I am writing this book for all Afrikans and people of Afrikan origin, whose culture has given so much to our global society. For instance, the basic values of how to relate to another human being originally came from Afrikans. But while we brought this gift to the rest of the world, at the moment we are failing to use it for ourselves in order to produce a great, modern Afrikan society.

Another reason why I believe that this book is critical is that Afrikans actually know that they are losing a lot by abandoning their culture. They know that every other culture that looks as if it is doing better than us, may be doing better than us in the area of making money, but is it successful at creating a peaceful, just and equitable society? Afrikans know that many of the so-called 'developed nations' are losing it. Even the most powerful country of our time, the United States of America, is losing it. You do not need to look further than television to see the levels of abuse and violence and the lack of tolerance around religion.

The other reason why this book is important at this time in our history is that you can take an Afrikan out of the village, but you cannot really take the village out of the Afrikan! So Afrikans know by instinct that we have the most efficient and most cost-effective social security system in the world: the family and extended family. The way in which our ancestors over the centuries crafted family and extended family structures was so well thought through, that it became practically impossible to have people who are totally destitute, so that they do not even have a home or a family. The extended family system as it used to be practiced across Afrika is the best system ever devised by any culture in dealing with social issues.

But Afrikans have been losing this brilliant system because they are trying to follow the Western way of life. The idea for us as Afrikans is not to Westernise, but to modernise our own society.

If the extended family system is under pressure because of the new environment, then we as Afrikans must reinvent it, rather than abandon it, or replace it with Western ideas. Let me explain: if you have a typically Western 'nuclear family', but the economy in which you live is not a Western economy, and governments are not the same as in the Western economy, you will be suffering.

Our ancestors knew long before modern-day scientists and genetic studies appeared, that your brother, your sister and you are practically 'one and the same'. They knew that your father's brother is your father; your mother's sister is your mother. In fact, they knew that all your mother's sisters – when you look at a cellular level using today's modern science – are your mothers. So their thinking was, why would you let your sister's child go destitute when you and her are one and the same: basically, your sister is you! Would you let your own child live on the street?

So when our ancestors crafted the extended family system they crafted a system, which would ensure that there would be love, peace and prosperity within the family, extended family and community in perpetuity - for all time... No social security system based on the Western model can provide this guarantee.

The fourth reason why this book is of critical importance as we enter the 21st Century is that we Afrikans, in spite of our physical poverty, are still the wealthiest people on the Earth when it comes to spirituality. So what we may lack in physical wealth, we overcompensate through our spiritual wealth. Where other cultures have neglected their spiritual development and connection to God in favour of physical things or socialist systems and simply focus on their mental ability, we Afrikans know instinctively that an important part of being human is our spiritual being. We know that when our bodies stop living, our spirit continues to exist.

However, we are faced with the problem that this wealth is also eroding, because most Afrikans are not aware of the fact that religion is the most important factor to keep any culture alive. And that religion ultimately determines how people approach life in all other spheres of life – whether it is business, how you look at justice, how you think about social issues, knowledge in general and how you grow the knowledge. So religion and culture both come from the same place. Culture is about how people live, how they behave, what are the accepted norms of living with others, of behaving towards others, of acting, of thinking and of communicating.

Religion, like culture, is deeply situated in assumptions and beliefs. Most of these are not tested. Actually, most of these are not even 'test-able': you cannot really know by way of scientific evidence what is true or false. So religion is about believing in things you cannot prove. But because of some other deeper senses that you have, you believe in those things anyway. And it is this faith that connects us with God. Ultimately, religion - as an attempt to connect us with God - may or may not form a rational basis or even be the best foundation for all the other cultural elements. But actually this does not really matter: any religion, as long as it connects someone to God, is performing a good function. The problem arises when one religion does not believe that other religions are legitimate or have a right to exist. The problem arises when one religion is seen as the only right one and others are seen as wrong.

Generally speaking, Afrikans have always known and believed in the existence of a greater God. And Afrikans have always known and believed that their connection with God is through our ancestors.

Here is why it is important to deal with the issue of religion in this book: colonialism, both by Islamic groups from the north into the North and East Coast of Afrika and soon afterwards by Christians in the South, resulted in Afrikans abandoning their own ancestor-based religion and adopting a doctrine-based religion. These doctrines taught us that you cannot believe in your ancestors and in God, and at the same time be a Christian or a Muslim. According to these faith systems, you cannot connect to God through your ancestors, only through Jesus Christ or Mohamed.

This was the single, biggest blow dealt to us Afrikans, because by destroying our religion, which was understood as the basis of our culture, it diluted our confidence in ourselves as a people. Both Arabic and European colonists believed that Afrikan knowledge and wisdom were inferior forms of knowledge compared to their own forms of knowledge. As a result, Afrikans were forced to choose a new culture and form of knowledge together with a new religion. This is a serious problem – even today: we as Afrikans have either lost or are in great danger of losing our cultural identity completely.

I want us as Afrikans to look at ourselves again and know that we have to be proud of our ancestors and the wealth of knowledge that they built for us over millions of years. We have to acknowledge that it is through our ancestors that we are here. And that our ancestors love us. It is through them that God allowed us to be here today. We can see our ancestors as the most direct connection, both physically and spiritually, between God and us.

I would go as far as saying that one day science is likely to prove that Afrikan ancestors were right all along, namely that your ancestors, or the ones who have brought you into this world, are the most direct connection between yourself and God. The logic is easy: if you follow the link from your mother, your father and the mothers and fathers who brought your mother and father into this world, and those before them, you have to end up at God.

According to Afrikan faith, you don't have to read a book to connect with God. Our ancestors believed that you don't have to convert other people from their religion or their belief in their God. Afrikans traditionally believed in their own ancestors as their connection to God, and were quite happy for others to have a different way of connecting to God. This way o thinking allows everyone to live peacefully next to one another.

But Afrikans that have adopted doctrine-based religions are in danger of becoming part of the international decay of spirituality, that may even result in a third world war or a fourth world war, as the followers of these doctrine-based religions seek to eliminate each other and become dominant.

Finally, I decided to write this book because I have a proposition to make to all Afrikans in terms of what I believe is the single most important idea that can help strengthen the regeneration and Afrikan renaissance in all areas of society. This idea, which is in the form of a general theory, can have a major significance in all spheres of Afrikan life, be it politics and party politics, government, business, economics, social integration issues, peace, security, prosperity, education and culture. I think it can help to explain why Afrikan society continues to break down. At the same time, the theory also explains how we can stop the decay and start rebuilding our beloved Afrika.

Chapter 1
A Young Shona Boy

I was born in the 1950's as a rural Afrikan Shona boy, in the Bikita District of Zimbabwe. Both my parents were trained as nurses. At the time I was born, they had retired from their nursing careers and had started a small business. So by and large they had a rural middle-class lifestyle. My parents were both Christians and members of the Dutch Reformed Church, which has since changed its name to the Reformed Church in Zimbabwe. At the same time, my parents were great believers in Afrikan tradition and the greater/extended family.

As a young person, I noticed several things. For instance, even as a child I became more and more aware that although it looked as if we Afrikans were regarded as backwards, we actually had a great past. Through the stories told in my own clan, which is the Rozvi clan within the Shona group, I learnt that there is a wealth of Afrikan history passed on by word of mouth from one generation to the next. These stories point at some of the great deeds of my ancestors from the past.

Probably the most significant historical achievement of my clan was their role in the establishment of the Empire of Great Zimbabwe, also known as the Monomotapa civilisation. It is estimated that the Empire existed from about 900 A.D. for more than six hundred years to the 1600s, and the Rozvi clan played an important part in driving out Portuguese colonists from the area during the late 1600s. The clan then remained in power until the early 1800s, when advancing Ndebele warriors took over the south-Western part of the former empire.

At its peak during the 1400s the Monomotapa civilisation extended its influence across a great geographical area spanning all of Zimbabwe, parts of Mozambique, South Afrika and Botswana. It had its headquarters at the site of the Great Zimbabwe Monument near Masvingo in south-eastern Zimbabwe. What made this civilisation unique was the integration of religion and politics to a level where certain principles of Afrikan traditional democracy became accepted practice throughout its area of influence. In addition, the civilisation had a great impact on the social and economic progress of its peoples, establishing economic relations with Arabs from North Afrika and the Middle East, as well as with the Chinese in the East.

But of course, when explorers from Europe discovered the abandoned site of these headquarters in the 19th century there was so much archaelogical evidence of a great civilisation, that it took the Europeans more than 50 years to start believing that this was built by Afrikans! Western literature is filled with early theories as to who might have built this civilisation outside of the Afrikan or Shona cultures, speculating that it must have been Arabic or Asian immigrants to Afrika. Fortunately, it is now clear to all the world that this was a Shona Afrikan civilisation. And that this civilisation at its peak was just as advanced as other enlightened cultures of its time in other parts of the world, such as the Incas of Latin America.

There is proof that Great Zimbabwe had all the major characteristics of an enlightened society: from organised religion, to economic progress, to peace and prosperity, as well as high regard for expressions of culture through art and music.

Today Shona stone sculpture is renowned internationally. Over the last 3 decades, several Zimbabweans have been cited amongst the top ten stone sculptors in the world. This is not an accident: stone sculpting as an art form is found etched deeply in the history and culture of the people, well before white colonists showed up.

For example, when early explorers from Europe discovered the Great Zimbabwe site, six stone carvings of the Zimbabwe Bird stood within the hill complex that makes up the temple site or religious site. The 'Zimbabwe Bird' is a mythical bird and the six stone carvings stood upright as part of the temple, just about the average height of a human being. These priceless pieces of art are relics that are now more than 1000 years old.

Because of the great political influence of the civilisation, miniature replicas of these stone houses are found right across the southern Afrikan region, including Mozambique and South Afrika. An important archaeological site, where such replicas were found, was discovered in 1932 in the Limpopo River valley at Mapungubwe in South Afrika. This site is linked directly to the Great Zimbabwe civilisation and valuable objects of art, including a famous gold-foil rhinoceros, have been found here. Mapungubwe is believed to have achieved its peak in the 13th Century.

The other distinguishing feature of the Rozvi political culture was a highly democratic approach to governance, which included dialogue processes, consultation and rotational leadership. The most important quality of any leader in this culture was their capacity to love their people and to then introduce processes and procedures that finally were aimed at uniting people.

Over the years I have learnt from other Afrikans that their clans also have great stories to tell about their own history. Having a legacy of greatness is not just limited to the Shona people. In different forms, other historic Afrikan civilisations developed across the continent. Because Afrika is the oldest continent in the world, it may be worthwhile for young Afrikans to consider becoming archaeologists. In this way we could uncover more scientific proof of the great achievements of the peoples of Afrika over the millions of years of their life on this continent.

But as a young person, I did not just learn from history, I also learnt through observation. For instance, I saw that because my parents were Christian we used to go to the Christian Church. However, most of the people in the community did not go to this church. They still practised ancestor-based religion. This was a big issue in my family. It was almost like saying, that you cannot be modern, have an education and be part of a prospering society if you still believe in ancestors. Instead, the thinking was that if you want to be successful you have to convert to Christianity and you have to go to a Western-style school to learn about God through the Bible and learn about life in a foreign language. So I could see how my parents and other middle-class people such as teachers were prospering because they could speak English and had a Western-style education.

But I could also see that life was a bit more complicated than that. I could see that there were good and bad people who were members of the Christian Church and that there were good and bad people in our community, who practiced ancestral religion. Later in life I looked back at my late father's life and personality. I asked myself why he was such great human being who loved his relatives and friends so much. Was it because he was a Christian? I concluded not; he was that good because he was a genuine Afrikan; although a Christian, the real foundation was his true *Unhu-Ubuntu-Botho* spirit.

The other thing that fascinated me is that I noticed that the church I went to with my parents was very, very boring. I remember we would go into this church and there would maybe be ten to twenty of us in this church. It was very difficult to listen to the preaching. Everything the pastor spoke about seemed so far away. The events he spoke about all happened almost 10 000km away. I was wondering if he was talking about us, or about other people. How did all of this have anything to do with me? So basically I thought that our church was really boring.

However, there was another Christian Church, to which my father's brother belonged. This was called the Zionist Christian Church (ZCC) and life at that church always looked much more exciting than at our church. As a result, my friends and I always looked forward to the end the church service, which - in a very Western manner - finished in exactly one to one-and-half hour, so that we could join the people at the ZCC. Here you would find 200-300 people, all singing and dancing and praising their God in a whole-day affair. At this church the people were using a similar way to the traditional Afrikan way of connecting to God, but they were doing this through Jesus Christ instead of through their ancestors. They were following the trend of having to go to a Western style church, but did it in a way that carried along their own culture. I later realised that this church was so big, it had a few million members. It really connected to Afrikan people, especially those from poor backgrounds. So as a young person I started asking myself a lot of interesting questions around religion.

As a young Afrikan I also became aware of issues around language. A foreign European language, English, had become the language of education and the language of the 'enlightened'. What this meant for me as a young person is that at home we spoke in Shona, then when we went to school, we had to speak in English. At school we were not allowed to speak in our mother tongue.

I also realised that the schools and the educational system had become one big system that created a bias towards leaving behind our own Afrikan culture and learning to live according to a Western culture. Schools were basically being used to wipe out our culture by teaching that the Western culture was more 'modern' and therefore more advanced. Even now, millions of youth who at home speak an Afrikan language and who learn a whole bunch of social skills, then have to leave this knowledge behind and go to school to learn a completely new way of life. So right there, from the early age of five when you enter pre-school, as an Afrikan child you are faced with a major clash between what you see, hear and learn at home and what you see, hear and learn at school.

As I write this book, I am deeply aware that I continue to carry this conflict around in me. This is not to say that all that we are learning at school is bad, because it is un-Afrikan! Some of the knowledge we are learning is very helpful, but the ongoing tension between the two forms of knowledge creates conflict. Instead of learning that we should select the best from both worlds, but build on our own culture, we are taught that our own culture is 'backward' and that only the Western way of life is useful in this modern day and age.

The older I became and the more I travelled in Afrika and in other parts of the world, the more I realised that there is something wrong in the way in which both a foreign language and a particular religion were forced upon me. I had grown up into an adult believing that my Afrikan roots and culture were a serious disadvantage and that my Afrikan religion and culture were the source of all the problems we have in Afrika! Of course, growing up with that frame of mind, you think that the solution is to abandon your 'Afrikan-ness' and to adopt everything that is Western.

I further realised that other parts of the world which were also as colonised by Europeans during the past 200-300 years as we Afrikans were, seemed to deal with this 'Western invasion' in a much more positive way. For instance, some of the people from Asia seemed to have found a way of seeing a difference between Western technology and Western culture. As a result, for example the Japanese have been better able to borrow Western ideas and technology and express them in their own culture, without losing their own religion or culture. In fact, they were borrowing so intelligently from the West, that the foreign technology would be improved by their own culture and religion. For instance, Japanese religion and culture has a principle of continuous improvement. They apply this principle to the technology they can access from the West. In this way they create a better product overall.

I also noticed as a professional person, that as an Afrikan professional, technician or career person, I was not as competent or as confident as the Asians have been in borrowing ideas intelligently, and then bringing them home, into the cultural context of my people. We have a joke in my circles where you say if you have an Asian going to Europe, they will 'borrow' the best ideas and technology, take them back to Asia, culturalise them and do better than the Europeans. If you send an

Afrikan professional like myself, then the best thing that is borrowed are European table manners! I have come to the realisation, that as an Afrikan professional who has been exposed to a large body of knowledge from outside of Afrika, I have not been able to convert that knowledge into a form that is useful for my people at home.

If we look a little closer at the Japanese, we will see that about 150 years ago they started borrowing intelligently from the West. This was about the same time when Europeans seriously started the colonisation of the whole of Afrika. The Japanese brought Western knowledge into their schools and industry, but they would convert that knowledge into Japanese language, so that they could teach their children the knowledge in their own mother tongue. The Chinese did the same. The result was that every Japanese and Chinese child could learn about these new ideas coming from another part of the world in their own language.

As an Afrikan, on the other hand, I find that I can only connect with my own people in my own language on certain levels. If I want to delve deeper into technology, for instance, I am unable to connect in my mother tongue. Because technology is so important in the times we are living in, it means that in this century the languages in which we can talk about this technology will be the medium of power. During the last two hundred years these languages were English,

French, German and Japanese. With the large number of Chinese speaking people in the world and China's speed of economic growth in recent years, it looks like the Mandarin language may well become another language of power in future. In Afrika, as in the majority of countries across the world, English - the language of Western capitalism - is really the language of power. The bulk of the people who cannot command English at higher level do not have much space to let their voices be heard in politics, science, technology and religion.

A short while ago, I was chatting to a Ghanaian friend of mine, Professor Kwesi Prah, one of the top Afrikan language specialists in the world today. He was telling me that it is impossible for any society to advance to a higher level through a foreign language. There is no society that has done so. Even in small nations that show relative economic success, such as Iceland, the medium of instruction is the mother tongue. So the young people speak the same language and practice their own culture at home, at school and at university. This means that they learn to translate knowledge they receive from outside into a useful form in their own culture. What we Afrikans have to learn from this is that we simply *have to* find a way of translating any knowledge that we find from outside our own culture into one or more Afrikan languages that are understood by the majority of people in Afrika. We need to be able to add cultural value to the knowledge we adopt and without interpreting that knowledge into an Afrikan language, this will remain almost impossible.

My friend Kwesi also shared a colonial joke from Ghana which shows the power of religion and language. Because we have been colonised through language and religion, we put the white man closer to God than us Afrikans in a single stroke: we believe that the white man brought God to us. So the colonial joke is that if on a Sunday morning you met a white man on the way to church, you might as well go home, because already you met God Himself on the way there!

I am raising this point, because I want to emphasise that it is really important for us as Afrikans to believe that our ancestors were always connected to God, they didn't need anyone else to connect to God. As a result, we should not believe ourselves to be 'inferior' to the white man, when it comes to our relationship with God. Our ancestors knew God well before any white person walked the Afrikan soil!

Today, Afrikans and diaspora people of Afrikan descent, confuse spirituality with religion. I won't go deep on this issue in this book though. In summary, however, spiritual growth is about deepening awareness of one's connectedness to other humans, and oneness with nature, and the omnipresent creative force out there that connects the whole universe. Religion, on the other hand, is a subscription to a specific faith paradigm, doctrine and related rituals and beliefs in God. In general, therefore, spirituality is a personal experience and religion is a group organised activity. Spirituality is inclusive of all; religion is about exclusive identity- - identifying with those of similar belief.

Why am I labouring this point? This book is ultimately about self-belief and self-identity of us Afrikans. As we lose our cultural identity and belief system, we flock to all sorts of churches in search of identity. Moreover, we are inherently a spiritual people and we used to practise this through *Unhu-Ubuntu-Botho*. As we lose this connection, we assume the church is the answer to spiritual growth. Think again.

While I started asking some questions as a young Shona boy, it is only as a professional and in my career that I started realising how wrong I was in underrating my culture and my religion. This realisation came as a great shock to me, because I had believed up to that time, that my Afrikan culture and Afrikan Religion were 'backward' compared to the West, because of their seemingly superior knowledge. By the time I started realising my misunderstanding, I had already published more than half a dozen books and maybe a hundred articles, all repeating my own gullibility in this regard! I was a world-renowned expert in three areas: food security issues for Afrika, economics of small-scale irrigation in Afrika, and on issues of land-tenure.

After being a lecturer at the University of Zimbabwe since 1980 I had been promoted to full professor in 1992. Then the following year, in 1993, I was appointed by Zimbabwean President Robert Mugabe to chair the Commission of Inquiry into Land Tenure Systems in that country. I started off in this temporary assignment, which I did for about 14 months, believing that the Afrikan tenure systems are a problem, because my formal Western education was telling me this. I firmly was of the opinion that we had to convert all of the traditional land-ownership systems into Western-style tenure systems, namely into leases and title deeds. I also believed that the traditional Afrikan system of land-ownership was dysfunctional.

Within six months of doing the land tenure work I realised how wrong I was in my thinking! By the time I had completed the exercise, I had visited 44 districts out of 56 in Zimbabwe. And in each district I had talked to all different groups and farmers, from the small-holder farmers, to the small-scale commercial farmers, to large-scale commercial white farmers, to people who had been resettled on land by government, including young people and women. At the end of this exercise I was deeply shocked by my ignorance about my own culture and my own people.

The biggest shock was that up until then I actually had believed that Afrikan culture and traditional beliefs and institutions were a thing of the past and merely a romantic issue. I was shocked to find that in fact they were alive and kicking, and that most Afrikans in rural areas believed strongly in traditional leadership and were largely disappointed with elected forms of leadership.

The other surprise for me was that after talking with civil society organisations and urban-based women organisations, I had also formed strong views regarding Afrikan culture as being gender insensitive and that everything was wrong with the way Afrikan culture deals with issues of gender, equity and democracy. To my surprise I found that in general both men, women, as well as young people in rural areas still preferred the traditional leadership systems in spite of any weaknesses, because they still provided them with more practical and accessible support systems, than the overrated 'modern' local government and related systems sponsored by government.

This is when I started realising that from the time of being a young Shona boy to being a young Afrikan professional I had been so consumed by Western concepts and Western knowledge, that I had become irrelevant to the situation in my own country. This was a major psychological blow to me. It was such a huge embarrassment for me, that I felt that the professorship which had been conferred to me 18 months earlier was almost fake.

It was really embarrassing and shocking to realise that I was regarded as a highly learned person, highly regarded in my society and even internationally, having written all these volumes of work, which were technically good, but the total paradigm of thinking was wrong. Up to that time I had been operating with a pattern of principles and ideas that was totally irrelevant to the reality on the ground.

This work confirmed a basic instinct that I had had for a long time. And that is, firstly, that Afrikan culture is one of the most pragmatic and most functional of any culture that I have seen anywhere else. It also confirmed to me that the basic paradigm of *Unhu-Ubuntu-Botho*, and how our ancestors used that framework to craft institutions such as family and community, was one of the most powerful paradigms in all of human civilisation.

In summary, Afrikan society was crafted over centuries, so that it is fully self-contained and functional at a local level. This means that all issues important in life are dealt with at the family and community level. As a result, all the major ingredients of a rich society such as religion, education, politics and governance, peace and conflict resolution, are dealt with first and foremost within the family and then within the community. Only after they have been addressed at this level, you start worrying about governments and all these higher level institutions.

So from about 1993 to 1994 I began to realise that the impact of the decay of Afrikan society, can be traced back to the decay of the family and community institutions that were developed by our ancestors over centuries.

For example, when you go into Afrikan rural communities today, you will find orphans that are destitute, with no homes or families to take care of them. You will find that some of them are taken care of by well-wishers, donor agencies, government institutions, or are being looked after by volunteer-mothers and fathers. Basically, they are taken care of by a whole bunch of unsustainable institutions.

I then asked myself the question: how is it possible that when our ancestors built an extended family system over centuries, which would make it impossible to have destitute children and old-aged people, that - within a space of thirty years - this whole institution has collapsed to this extent? Can HIV/AIDS account for this calamity or has AIDS been but a last straw on an already crumbling backbone of the greater/extended family system?

The answer is obvious: it is because over the last one hundred years or so, Afrikans started to abandon what their ancestors had created for them and started to adopt Westernised ideas of the 'nuclear family', of individualism and independence.

In fact, this was bothering me so much, that one day - it was in March 2006 - I simply lost my temper! I was staying at a hotel in Bulawayo in Zimbabwe, for a meeting aimed at discussing broader issues of rebuilding Afrikan communities. In the morning when I got up, I saw a copy of the daily newspaper under my door. I picked it up and on the front page of that paper was the most infuriating picture. This picture was in full colour – showing a visiting white man who was a vice-president of an international aid organisation, seated in a chair and surrounded by about half-a-dozen Afrikan men and women seated in their chairs, each one holding an orphan in their lap. The message of the picture was that these Afrikans were showing their gratitude to the international aid organisation for all the support they were getting to take care of these orphans. What infuriated me was, that my own ancestors, over the years, had created a system that would ensure that even in situations of extreme poverty, there would be no need for a single destitute orphan or child. Even in situations of extreme poverty, orphans would share that situation with their brothers and sisters in their greater family. Now, in less than thirty years, we have a situation where we Afrikans need an international organisation and a white man flying in from Europe, to help us look after our own orphans! To me this means that instead of going forward through Westernisation, as a culture we have gone backwards a couple of centuries!

I still have this picture. I carry it around in my bag as a reminder of this insight so that I can share it with fellow Afrikans.

When you look at the general problem of fragmentation we have in Afrika, you could say that what has happened since colonisation over the last century or so, is a continuous erosion of the capacity of families and communities to handle issues and challenges that were initially handled by family, extended family and community. Family, extended family and community were the key three institutions that would take care of culture, education, religion, conflict resolution, justice system, gathering of knowledge and sharing it, politics, self-governance – it was all contained in those three institutions.

Today, those three institutions have been eroded largely through the establishment of nation-states as a new Western idea. These new nation-states - all of which have borders decided upon by European colonizers - have a complete disregard for the need to have strong families and strong communities. In fact, it is so bad in some parts of Afrika, that the new Afrikan-led nation-states prefer it that way. They know that if you do not have strong extended families, then you do not have strong clans, and as a result you do not have strong linguistic or local communities that could question what is happening at the national level!

When families and communities in Western countries fail, their functions are replaced by the government. So in Western countries the governments worry about everything that used to be dealt with at individual, family and community level. However, Afrika does not have the resources to have police and courts of law in every village. So the general problems in Afrika are only going to be solved by rebuilding the family, the extended family and the community and to re-establish strong values of *Unhu-Ubuntu-Botho* within that group of institutions. Only then, once again, hunger and malnutrition, housebreaking and domestic violence, crime and all the illnesses today, can be dealt with within the family and community structures. The role of the state would then be to support these institutions, rather than to carry the major burden.

After all, the most important thing that Afrikans have, that others don't have to the same extent, is our understanding of the importance of relationships between humans and the ability to maintain them.

As an Afrikan I would like to say to my fellow Afrikans, I don't think in the short term we will or have to beat the Western world in terms of technology – we just have to borrow intelligently. I don't think we will or have to surpass the Asians, in particularly the Chinese, in process engineering and production, we can also borrow intelligently from them. But where we as Afrikans will lead the world, and accelerate our own ability, is through our understanding of people and relationships.

We Afrikans have to continue to show the world, what it means to be a human being – what happiness really means in life. This we can only do through our heritage, that is *Unhu* or *Ubuntu*: love for God, love for one another, and bringing to ourselves and the rest of the world music, sport, arts and other forms of expression which bring out the best of the human spirit and connects people across the boundaries of material life. These assets, which transcend culture and language – that is where our strength as Afrikans lies.

Chapter 2
Afrika's Forgotten Treasure

If I remember the date at all it must have been 2003 that I was flying back from the United States of America to Afrika. At Heathrow Airport I took a day room while waiting for the connecting flight to South Afrika. I was watching television and trying to catch up with myself. Then the popular Oprah Show came on. This day Oprah had invited Billy Crystal as a special guest and he was there to talk about family and relationships. The highlight of his story was how he looked for the only surviving brother of his father – his uncle. He had not known this man well while growing up, and his own father had died when this famous actor and comedian was still very young.

Billy Crystal was talking about the joy of going out there to look for his father's brother, and eventually finding him. He spoke about how his father's brother was telling him stories about the family, including about his dad. Billy Crystal and Oprah were sharing the message of the importance of connectedness between family and loved-ones. They were talking about the deep memories, institutional memories, and heritage that comes with having strong family ties.

I watched this conversation because I know Billy Crystal from TV and love him as a highly successful comedian. However, I was sitting and looking at the screen in disbelief, thinking that this is the Oprah show being watched by millions of people across the world – and Billy Crystal is telling the world how he rediscovered his father's brother, as an old man! I could not help thinking to myself that if Oprah was to come to Afrika, all of us would end up on her show, especially me, because I have countless fathers, mothers, uncles and aunts that I could tell stories about!

I grew up in an environment where I was connected to so many relatives. My father's brothers were all fathers to me, my father's cousins were all fathers to me. For me, each one of them brought a different value, which enriched my life. If I wanted to go hunting, I knew which father to ask to take me along. If I had trouble with women, I knew from which father to get advice. If I wanted to learn a certain craft or skill, there was someone who could mentor me.

So there I am sitting, looking at Billy Crystal on Oprah, talking about finding only one of his fathers and this late in his life when he is a successful man already! So I said to myself, if this is where we are going to, if it is going to take me as an Afrikan to be successful and only then to start worrying about my family, then we are in deep trouble. For me, the essential importance of family is a practical issue, not just a theoretical one.

This is not just because of the traditional foundation, which our ancestors crafted, but it is still today the only base, which we as Afrikans have on which to build a modern Afrikan society. The ability to build great relationships with one another and strong families, and through that, strong communities is the 'Forgotten Treasure' that Afrikans own. We need to dig deep into the garden of our ancestral memory to uncover this incredible source of wealth that will help us move ahead as a strong and successful continent.

For Afrikans the boundary between family and greater/extended family is theoretical. When we talk about family, we always mean the greater/extended family. Maybe we can talk about a household, if we want to refer to a certain group of people sharing a living space. But households are only a minor building block of the overall family.

Family is important, because that is both the space and the place in which you initially experience all the ingredients of self-belief and identity.

There is no crisis in a human being that is bigger than the crisis of loss of identity. Humans love to belong. They crave a sense of belonging and a sense of connectedness with others. This sense of belonging and connectedness starts within the family. If someone loses the sense of belonging within his or her family, and tries to later in life recreate it, it is very difficult to be a happy person. Often they try and belong to some gang, church or another poor substitute.

This is why my message to my fellow-Afrikans and even my fellow human beings everywhere else is, that we are better off through connectedness to our families from an early age, than to focus on a career goal and then try to connect to them afterwards. This is what has killed and is still killing our society.

Family is a space where Afrikans created the concept of relationships. And then perfected it to best practice over the centuries.

Families start first and foremost with blood-relatives. Next you include the relatives of blood-relatives, who may not be your own blood-relatives. The we get to in-laws, friends and neighbours and all of these form and bond into clans and, or communities.

Another 'Forgotten Treasure' that Afrikans can revive is the use of the totem and clan names. Most Afrikans are proud of their totem and clan names. I have yet to meet an Afrikan who does not feel deeply proud if you call them by their totem or clan name. For instance, my totem is '*Moyo*◻ *Moyo* is Shona for 'heart' and refers to people who have a 'long heart', meaning a fundamentally positive attitude to life. My clan name is '*Moyondizvo*◻ This name comes from *Moyo* and means

49

'the real *Moyo* people' so as to distinguish our clan from other Moyo people.

If you look at it from a modern perspective, the totem and the clan name are some of the most powerful brands in Afrikan society. For instance, if you want a comparison to understand the totem and clan name in a modern-day setting, we can compare 'Moyondizvo' to 'Coca-Cola'. I love Coca-Cola and it is one of the strongest brands in the world today. But if you would ask me to choose between Coca Cola and Moyondizvo, I would not hesitate for a second which brand to support: Moyondizvo, of course! The Coca-Cola brand is worth millions of dollars. As Afrikans, we need to appreciate the value of our totem and clan name brands.

Afrikans understood the essence of branding – cultural branding – well before we were colonised or exposed to the principle of capitalism. The importance of the cultural or clan 'brand' is that it bestows upon one in an instant all the heritage of your ancestors. This is a way of knowing that before I even achieve anything with my life and in myself, I already own all the major achievements of my ancestors. I carry within me the celebration of their successes and the lessons of their failures, but above all, I am here to continue the great deeds of my people. I am not just an 'accident of nature', planted on earth in isolation and without purpose. I am the result of an age-old chain of relationships and proof that - since the very beginning of time - my ancestors were strong enough to survive the worst of challenges that life on earth had to offer. This means that I have access to a lasting resource, a source of wealth - like knowledge or a skill - that no one can take away from me. I carry within me a sense of identity that gives me a deep sense of self-confidence because I have an automatic sense of belonging.

This sense of belonging starts within the family. And so does the sense of connectedness to God. Both of these lay the foundation for each individual to own a strong sense of purpose: our purpose as Afrikans is firstly, to continue to strengthen our relationship to God, and secondly, to build on the great deeds of our ancestors.

Also, the family is a social unit, which prepares all of us from a tender age for a full life. Through our family we learn how to develop relationships with others, how to think and find solutions together with others, how to make ideas happen and work with others. And of course, how to share feelings with others – whether these feelings are about joy, sorrow, triumph or defeat. It is important to go through all these actions and feelings together with family. This is what prepares us for the bigger things in life. The skills needed to make an Afrikan family function effectively and efficiently, are the same skills that are needed to run a community, a business, a country and a continent.

In Afrikan family and religion the roles and responsibilities of each member are very important. After all, role-playing is the order of the culture: we learn to play different roles and put ourselves in the 'other's' shoes from a very early age onwards. This means that all of us play all the other family roles at different points in time. The exact roles and responsibilities and how they are carried out are different from one Afrikan cultural group to another, but having different roles within an extended family is a common thread running through all different cultural groups in Afrika.

For example, for me as a member of the Shona people, although I am a man, I play all the various roles within the greater extended family. As a man I play a role as a husband. I am also a father, both for my own children, as well as for the children of my brothers. But for my sister's children, I play a role as a male mother! Because to them I am a male mother, I have to step in as their mother and play the role of their mother, whenever there is a time that calls for that role.

To all my mother's sisters and cousins, I am their child. So it doesn't matter if one of my mother's cousins is twelve years old, while I may be 53 years old. I still treat that twelve year old child as my mother and I still play a role as a child to her – even in my late adult age. And she is expected to represent my mother and treat me as her child in the event that all the other mothers are absent or deceased.

Another common thread weaving through all Afrikan cultural groups is that the mother is central to the household. This is true in both in patrilineal, as well as in matrilineal systems. The mother is central. There is no home without a mother. In Afrikan traditional systems, a man cannot be allocated land or a home, if there is no wife, because it is the mother that is central to the household. For Afrikans, mothers are always closer to God than Fathers, because of the life-giving role they play.

As a result, abuse to women is not at all in line with traditional and historical values of Afrikans. In fact, I personally grew up in a family where I was told from a tender age, that abusing a woman was the most despised form of weakness. As a result, it was acceptable to intervene if another man was being abusive of a woman. I could even intervene with my father, and in severe cases even reprimand my father, if he was physically abusing my mother or another woman. However, I could not do this to my mother, because she was next to God, and she was more likely to overreact or make a mistake out of love and therefore to be forgiven.

Another characteristic found across traditional Afrikan family systems, is that decision-making is through a consultative process. This consultation may take different forms, depending on the issue at hand. For instance, in some issues consultation may only take place between the parents, while at other times consultation will include all children. Sometimes consultation is only between the parents and the adult children.

The husband is generally the head of the household, so this is a role he is supposed to play. However, in Afrikan families, this is not an executive role. In fact, in an Afrikan household the man is not supposed to dictate or even take most of the decisions. If a decision has to be taken, the greater part of the voice is given to the mother of the family, because she is more likely to understand the issues at home. But once the decision has been made, the father as the nominal head of the family, is expected to uphold the decision and communicate it outside the family. He is also responsible for protecting the integrity of the decision, thereby maintaining the integrity of the household.

Let me use an example from my own childhood. My mother and father would sit down to make a decision to allocate resources. My mother would have more to say, because she is the one that has to execute the decision. However, if the decision has something to do with someone outside the home, when my father is communicating the decision to someone outside, he is expected to communicate this as his own decision. The role of the male head of the household is to communicate decisions taken within the household, keep the integrity of the household intact and defend the decision from outside criticism.

The general tendency is for men, who are involved in activities outside the home, to bring those issues into the household for discussion. Because they are more involved in the interaction with the outside world, their opinion may count more in this regard. However, those external issues should always be discussed openly with the wife, and where applicable, with the family, because they may ultimately have an impact on the household.

So if the husband is working outside, or is hunting or has started a business, all processes related to his work, the hunting trip or the business have to brought back into the household and the wife is supposed to help think through how this is going to affect the household. Where both husband and wife are working outside of the household, both should bring the issues they are faced with outside of the home back into the household for discussion. By sharing the kinds of problems they have to deal with at work, in their individual social activities or in their business with the family, they are helping to build the capacity of all members of the family or at least of their spouse, to effectively address similar issues in future.

If Afrikan couples would do this in modern times, we would have the ability to address all kinds of problems, including HIV/Aids, extra-marital affairs, and the like.

After all, even though having many wives, or poligamy, was culturally very acceptable in most of Afrika, today, because of Western influence, it is not as publicly acceptable. So what then happens is that extra-marital affairs are not declared, leading to all sorts of social problems and HIV/Aids. In the past a man could only have or marry another wife, after the family agrees to the proposition. As a matter of fact, the existing wife or wives would have to sanction that decision, because after all they would be faced with another addition to the household. Secret extra-marital affairs were not at all acceptable!

Because of the apparent difference with the West and biblical interpretations of Christians, the issue of polygamy is swept under the carpet. However, you don't have to go very deep into the Western world to see that the marital system adopted in Western culture is under huge pressure. For instance, in the United States of America, more than half of the marriages end up in divorce. This means that even on your wedding day you have to face the reality that your romantic marriage has a greater chance of failing, than of continuing 'till death do you part'.

In the United States of America, despite the solemn vows taken in front of God at the altar, it has become quite acceptable, both in law and religion, to have as many marriages as you want, as long as the marriages neatly follow one another. From my perspective, this is serial polygamy. It is naïve to believe that after one marriage has ended and you go on to the next one, the relationship established in the first marriage no longer exists! You still have to relate to the ex-wife or the ex-husband, because of the children and the assets and the social upheaval is just as bad, often worse, than in dysfunctional parallel polygamous systems. In fact, in functional parallel polygamous systems, the rights of the former spouse and the children born of the marriage are generally better protected than in Western-style serial polygamy.

If you ask me which is better, serial polygamy or parallel polygamy, I would say neither is better or worse. After all, time and space are merely attributes of the physical world. At a spiritual level, just as it is at the quantum level, things are, and there is no real difference in meaning between events occurring in sequence as opposed to occurring all at once! Time chronology and physical space have no intrinsic value at the spiritual level. There is therefore no need for an agonizing debate between different marriage systems of the world. There is no basis on which one culture can lecture or preach to another on marriage. There is arranged marriage, as opposed to the courting romantic approach. Then there is serial versus parallel polygamy. And so on. It is all about cultural beliefs and value judgements, otherwise reality is such that there is both bliss as well major disaster in every marriage system.

It does seem, however, that a culture that promotes openness about the issue through its laws, its religion and in its cultural practices is a society that is better off. That is why Islamic societies, which declare parallel polygamy up-front, and those North-European societies, where these issues are faced openly, are probably better off in terms of HIV/Aids than Afrikan, South Asian or South American societies, which do not yet deal with these issues in an open manner.

Back to the bottom line: all the important ingredients of life are contained in the way the family functions. At community level, we are only working on a larger scale of how the family functions. Politics, religion and how we govern ourselves as a collective become more important at an aggregate level.

The Afrikan system of dealing with issues, which starts at family level, is known in Shona language as 'dare□ In other southern Afrikan languages this is described as 'tinkundla□ 'lekotla□ 'imbizo□ or 'indaba□ and refers to an agreed way of people sharing knowledge and making decisions that have an impact on all of the parties involved. The principles of 'dare' or 'indaba' are important to uphold at both family and community level. They become more important at community level, because the broader community comprises different families and extended families, some of which may not have blood relationships. But the principle of strong relationships is still maintained at community level.

In Afrikan tradition '*Dare*' is a universally acceptable medium for learning, sharing wisdom, for planning, addressing common issues and challenges in the community, conflict resolution, as well as collective action with the aim to promote peace and prosperity.

The principles of *Dare* include inclusiveness, meaning that all affected parties are included. Secondly, consultation is another principle. There is no issue, big or small, which can be ratified or confirmed in the bigger space before thorough consultations take place in that community. The third principle is dialogue. Our ancestors perfected the art of high-level dialogue. They believed so much in dialogue, that there was no issue big or small, that would be abandoned just because people had run out of time. Dialogue had to continue on an issue, if necessary, on and off, even over a long period of time, until a resolution had been reached.

Another principle is consensus-decision-making. Most decisions at community-level in Afrikan tradition are reached by consensus. Using dialogue, consultation and including more and more people, some with knowledge, some with wisdom, some with creative ideas, an issue is discussed until consensus is reached. The reason for this is that if consensus is reached, the decision is likely to be embraced by the greater community and has a better chance of being executed effectively.

So in Afrikan traditional politics, reaching consensus is much more preferred, than getting a majority vote.

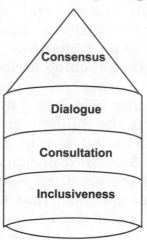

Fig. 1: The Building Blocks of a successful Afrikan Family, Community, Country and even Continent

The challenge that we face at community level is that all these consultative and consensus-building processes are being put aside in favour of elections. And, as we Afrikans know, issues are dynamic and complex. Merely rushing to get a vote does not always produce the best solution. Our ancestors also knew that. Quite often, the majority can be wrong. So why not thoroughly discuss an issue, until consensus is reached? This forms a much better basis for lasting solutions to challenges facing communities.

One important thing to point out it that in using the *dare* approach in resolving political and leadership issues, is that leaders do not rule! Leaders preside over processes. Leaders uphold the integrity of a system. Leaders are there to build trust and ownership in the political processes. They are not there to make a decision or to rule over others.

The challenge that we see today at community level is that we have Afrikan governments who prefer elections above building strong community systems. They would rather build election booths and register people for voting, than they would spend time building a system for strong community consulting and consensual decision-making processes. As a result, local government is weak, dysfunctional and unable to deliver for most people.

The challenge therefore is how to modernise family and community systems so that we rebuild the traditional processes as the main basis for local politics and governance.

Strong family systems are the Forgotten Treasure that Afrikan's need to rediscover from the past, redesign to make them relevant to the modern times we live in and recreate in order to enable strong communities.

Chapter 3
Building the House Backwards

If I had the opportunity to have an informal chat to Afrikan government leaders under a tree in my village, I would say to them: "Excuse me friends, the way I see it you are really trying to build the house backwards". Governments in Afrika are struggling to put a roof on a very weak and crumbling foundation. But instead of increasing their efforts to first get the foundation right, they show no interest in strengthening or building these institutions of family or community. Instead, they continue to throw money at cumbersome national structures that really have no means of reaching the individual or the community. In fact, there is a dangerous disconnect between the two: people on the ground are looking with suspicion at this 'roof' that is floating over them like an 'Unidentified Foreign Object', an UFO, filled with bureaucrats that seem rather alienated from the actual needs at community level.

In fact, this approach is not exclusive to governments in Afrika. The corporate sector is suffering from the same shortsightedness. Look for instance at the Financial Services Sector. The majority of people they are serving is an Elite that is simply just the tip of the population pyramid. Needless to say, the paradigm of fear is defining the viewpoint of many of these so-called global multinationals. From their birds' eyeview, they see an ever growing sea of poverty and crime that is threatening their future. If they could take the time and have the courage to go down from their precarious position in the clouds, they could see the other side of the coin: seemingly endless possibility!

I believe that if we want to see an Afrikan Renaissance, we first have to recreate the family and community, on the principles described in the previous chapter. Parallel to this, the same values and principles have to be applied to the rest of the nation. In other words, local government, central government, political parties, civil society structures, business entities all need to go back and apply the broad 'dare□principles that allow for social integration. No political party in Afrika should be allowed to function or even govern a nation, if it doesn't adhere to the principles of inclusiveness (acceptance of diversity and differences), consultation, open dialogue, consensus decision-making and tolerance. These are the principles that should be infused in the entire system of political and governance processes, all the way up to parliament and cabinet, including in particular also the police and the army, so that we can have strong society-building processes beyond the often dubious mathematics of elections.

Recent history in Afrika has sadly proven that as soon as our heroic 'grass-root' liberation movements have led their people into regaining political independence from Europe, they immediately seem to forget their roots and the real structure of their Afrikan society. Instead, they suddenly develop a new-found love for and focus on building a national government, either because of the political power it represents or because of a misunderstood and patronising role of having to establish a 'delivery system' on a national level for houses, jobs or education to what they see as a citizenry that is too helpless to build their own homes, create own income opportunities or provide relevant education to their own children!

Ironically, they then go so far as to try to recreate states resembling those of their former enemy: Europe. In addition, they also import the dominant Western culture of North America, treading the 'hidden treasure' of an own indigenous culture underfoot. In doing so, they end up working hand in glove with our former oppressors to continue with the process of colonisation of our minds by forcing foreign ideas and ways of doing things on us. The end result is that our liberators actually continue to place us in a position of economic dependency on the West. The irony is that because they have changed from political liberators into immensely popular political parties, no one dares to question our new, powerful leaders.

The other irony is that our liberation movements stopped at the borders drawn with a pen across the map of Afrika by the colonists, instead of working together across these borders to rejoin the large numbers of families that were violently separated by colonialist boundaries. Most of these boundaries don't make sense. Not only do they cut through the various clans and tribes, but they also create a further distance between peoples who are otherwise one, by invariably forcing them to communicate through a foreign language, thereby further alienating them from their own people!

For instance, the Manica Shona speakers in the Manica Province of Mozambique, are cut away from their Manica sisters and brothers on the Zimbabwean side. The official language for education of the former is Portuguese, while the language used on the side of the latter country is English. This separation of people of the same clan through an artificial national border and an official foreign language is replicated all over Afrika.

The question is, how does this all relate to national politics and nation building?

As I mentioned before, the biggest problem we have in Afrika today is that each and every country, without exception, is being build backwards: from the top down, from the roof to the foundation!

We Afrikans have been brainwashed so badly, and we continue to brainwash ourselves, into believing that we are going to build strong nation-states based on crumbling family and community structures. In fact, almost every government is doing its fair share of damage in destroying families and communities, clans and tribes, eliminating differences and diversity, in a feeble attempt to create the fiction of a nation-state, which simply does not exist.

A geographic demarcated area is not enough to build a sense of togetherness. Every national boundary on the Afrikan continent is nothing but a very recent random line drawn on a map as our colonial invaders fought among one another to cut out their own claim on the Afrikan continent. Our politicians and heads of states in Afrika have to remember that the political boundaries that exist today are left over from a colonial time, which continues to promote the original imperialistic intention to divide Afrikans with the aim to make it possible to dominate Afrika from the outside. Looking at the continued fragmented approach to international relations between the leaders of different countries in Afrika and the trade partners from other parts of the world, this is a very effective strategy! Also, it will remain effective as long as we as Afrikans do not commit ourselves to standing together, but try to negotiate individual benefits that do not serve the whole of Afrika.

Most Afrikans, communities and people, tribes, clans and broader cultural groups exist beyond national boundaries. It is absurd that the Afrikan Union continues to push the issue of statism, that is to emphasise the separateness of individual states, while breaking down the glue that will bind Afrika together, namely to relate to one another beyond the current political boundaries. As a modern-day Afrikan I am really surprised at how naïve Afrikan political parties and politicians have become, by not seeing what it takes to really build Afrika and not opening it up to enjoy the cultural, economic and natural diversity of the continent. We have really gone back at least one hundred years in our development. Even my own grandparents were still able to migrate freely throughout the continent, just one hundred years ago!

Our ancestors' ability to move freely across the continent is what made Afrikans develop and succeed faster than what we are doing today: culturally, politically and socially.

I am a southern Afrikan and even today I can go to parts of southern Afrika where there are people who closely resemble me physically and speak languages that are very similar to my own mother-tongue. They think I am one of them! But they live in a country where the government expects me to get a visa, before I can visit them.

The same thing happens when I go to East and West Afrika. This means that the richness of Afrikan culture today and the prominence of relationships is the most important social glue at all levels. In fact, as we travel across Afrika today, one can tell that as our ancestors migrated in many different directions, going back and forth and crisscrossing the continent several times, they still left behind a strong web of social relations which we could have used to build strong relationships across the continent. There are differences, but broadly speaking the cultural and social elements allow for great social integration and shared social capital.

This makes the idea that we are spending so much of our resources nowadays trying to uphold the idea of a nation-state truly ridiculous! This foreign idea imposed on Afrikans from the outside has put a stop to the natural migration in and out of the different regions of Afrika, which was a privilege that all people in Afrika had in the past. Surely, God never intended the world to be cut up into nation states to which other humans had no right of access? This is a modern-day result of very greedy, narrow-minded and selfish political thought across the world.

All the peoples of this world are migrant groups, regardless of where we are at this very moment. We all migrated from somewhere. It makes no sense to me that this world will be a better place in a thousand years through continuous restraint of movement and through violent and physical obstruction of people to relate and inter-relate across cultural groups, continents and political boundaries.

As an Afrikan I can confidently say that because the human race was established first on this continent through the transformation of ape-like creatures into human beings, every human being today traces his or her ancestry back to those early humans in Afrika. Since it was God's wish that we progress from apes to humans, and then spread over time throughout the world, I cannot see that it is either the wish of our ancestors, nor the wish of God, that millions of years later humans are confined in boxes. This narrow-minded nationalism and state-building is making it increasingly difficult for all human beings to freely intermingle and fulfill the global desire for peace, progress and freedom. In fact, it is these absurd nationalistic boundaries that, together with ethnic and religious fanaticism, have led to all these world wars and continues to fuel conflict across the world.

In conclusion, I truly believe that it will understandably be difficult to achieve sustainable peace, progress and freedom in a world where such restrictions continue to exist. The gradual melting away of these artificial political boundaries could be a great contributor to sustainable peace, progress and freedom of human beings in Afrika, as well as in the rest of the world.

Chapter 4
Afrikan Pathways of Being Human

In the previous chapter I emphasised the incredible wealth that we as Afrikans have, but - like someone who keeps the family silver in a cupboard for the odd special occasion - we sit on this treasure instead of enjoying its benefits to the full every day.

I have been criticising our governments in Afrika, for trying to build a house from the roof down. The same applies to each one of us, if we try to build a strong family, but ignore the fact that a family is made up of individuals. That is why I want to spend the next part of this book to share the ideas that our Afrikan ancestors used over time to grow strong, effective, individuals, as well as families and communities.

Families can only be as strong as the individuals in the family. The family creates the individual and the individual creates the family. This co-creation process is central to the way *Unhu-Ubuntu-Botho* or 'humanism' is experienced and employed as a way of life in Afrikan tradition. 'I am because we are.' Each one of us is the product of the people that have shaped our lives. To be human, we need these relationships with other human beings and the family context has the most impact on us as we grow into young adults and in turn help shape our family and its fortunes.

Unhu-Ubuntu-Botho comprises several pathways as a way of life, while at the same time developing strong families, communities and therefore strong, modern Afrikan nations. These age-old pathways have been developed to empower the individual, so that every single Afrikan man and woman has the ability to carry the responsibility for his or her life, family and community and the power to help chart the way of the continent of Afrika into the future.

In this book, I am describing the Shona interpretation of these pathways. However, from my visits to countries across Afrika, and from my discussions with people from all walks of life in these different countries, I am confident that the basic principles that guide each of the pathways are found in one form or another among Afrikan cultural groups all over the continent.

The *Unhu-Ubuntu-Botho* pathways have existed from times immemorial. The challenge before us is to continue to interpret them and continue to re-interpret them, so that they remain current and relevant to our situation as it changes. That is why it is important to treat these ten pathways as a way of life. At the same time it is necessary that we adjust the practical implications of these pathways at the 'speed of life' in a modern context.

Through adopting these pathways, we can speed up the process of the real Afrikan Renaissance, which is already happening. Initially, it will be more obvious at the individual level, later this rebirth will be expressing itself in broader society. But the bottom-line is: transformation in terms of peace, prosperity and freedom in Afrika will have to start with the individual.

I have learnt that I cannot change the world, if I do not first start changing myself. Using a quotation from Mahatma Gandhi, each one of us has to 'be the change' that we want to happen! In fact, I have learnt that the quickest way for me to help transform my own situation is by developing a greater and greater capacity to change and to reinvent myself within the situation that I am faced with, using the ten broad pathways as my guiding light.

So while this book introduces some thoughts about the future of our beloved continent of Afrika, it really is aimed at you as an individual. It is intended to change your view of what it is going to take for us to co-create the Afrika we want.

It will take a higher level of consciousness on the part of individual human beings for us to eventually generate the force that is necessary to achieve the transformation needed at family, community and national levels. This higher level of consciousness will take us beyond the need for independence to the celebration of our inter-dependence as human beings: I am, because we are!

Chapter 5
Know where you come from

The First Pathway:
Ziva kwawakabva

Know where you come from, know and respect your family, relatives and your ancestors.

O ur ancestors seem to have been smarter than us. They knew that the Spirit of God is eternal and has always existed, before the physical universe was created and before time was created.

Our ancestors also knew that the Spirit of God has kept itself moving along and passed over into all of God's creations. In human beings, the Spirit of God passed on to us through our ancestors.

So to know my father and my mother and to love and respect them is to know, love and respect God. Our ancestors also knew that our parents and their parents before them, that is our ancestors, are the most direct physical and spiritual connection that we as human beings have with God.

Before you can move forward in life with strength, confidence and courage, you have to know where you come from. You have to know, and continually be curious, about your roots.

As an Afrikan you have a totem and clan name. It is important for you to know your totem and clan name as the basis on which you dig into the history of your family and your people. Because of Afrika's oral tradition, it has been easy to lose a lot of knowledge and wisdom. Our ancestors believed strongly in oral tradition as a means of education. It is therefore important for us modern Afrikans to ensure that we educate ourselves and tell the stories about our families and our histories to our children.

In fact, there are a number of things that you have to do all the time in order to bring your own family heritage to life. Firstly, you have to memorise and repeat your clans' praise poetry. Within the praise poetry is contained, in summary form, a lot of evidence and information on your family's history. This is a celebration of the achievements of your ancestors.

The second thing is to know and love the different relatives you have within your extended family. It is important to keep up and maintain personal relationships with various members of your family, as well as with their friends and relatives.

Our ancestors believed that you have to love your relatives unconditionally. This means that you should never forsake your relatives and close friends, even in times of deep crisis or conflict. Teach your children and educate them on all the important relatives in your family. The Shona saying is that *'kuziva mbuya huudzwa*, meaning 'to know Grandmother is to have knowledge'. Today, we Afrikans assume that children should just find out for themselves who their relatives are. We assume that they should make their own time to establish meaningful relationships with other family members.

This does not work!

Learning about their family has to be part and parcel of the upbringing of any Afrikan from a young age. They have to establish contact, and maintain a good relationship with their grandparents, their cousins, and with other various types of relatives. It is very important that from a young age, our children learn to play the different roles expected in an extended family, of being a father, a mother, an uncle, aunt and various forms of relationship which are role-played in order to ensure that every human is equal and is expected to play different roles at different times. This is the best possible preparation for building successful relationships with people from all walks of life and finding win-win solutions later: role-playing teaches us to place ourselves in the shoes of the other. What better preparation than this to be able to switch perspectives quickly and find mutually beneficiary solutions to the challenges that face us later in life?

Love and respect your parents unconditionally. This is important because in adult life when you have your own family, you will expect to be loved by your children unconditionally, irrespective of your own shortcomings.

My experience is that if in your younger age you have disrespect for your own parents, in adult life your friends and spouse are likely to only respect you to the extent that you respected your own family. This is so in times of conflict or disagreement with your own spouse and friends.

That is why it is important, as part of *being*, to know where you come from. Remind yourself all the time that your ancestors and your God are always with you. Every moment of your existence is a culmination of what your ancestors and God bestowed upon you. Therefore, their spirit is with you always, all the time. This also helps you to remain connected to God all the time. After all, your ancestors are closer to God, because they knew God before you and after their departure are even closer to God in spirit.

So, our ancestors and therefore you and me, do not need anything else to establish a strong connection with God. We don't need to read clever books. We don't need to be preached to by another human being. All human beings are equal in the eyes of God. You are not above anybody. You are not below anybody either. No one has a monopoly of knowledge of God. It is therefore important for us as Afrikans in re-establishing our confidence and our self-knowledge, to know that our ancestors and our God are always with us and we don't need any other spiritual connection.

Chapter 6
Know where you are going

The Second Pathway:
Ziva kwaurikuenda

**Know where you're going and
fulfil the gifts that your God bestowed on you.**

Now that you know where you come from, and through prayer continually reconnect with the source of your life in order to boost your spirit and courage, you are better prepared to know where you are going and to achieve great things with your life.

Life is a journey and not a destination. It is more important in life to be happy and to pursue worthwhile activities.

The question is how do you move forward to achieve happiness and purposeful occupation? How do you know what career to pursue, what kind of life you would like to lead? My experience is that, in order to answer all these important questions about your life, it is important to accept ahead of time that this can only be solved through a process of self-discovery.

There are so many things you could do with your life. And it is not always easy to decide which path to take. The wisdom from our ancestors is that there broadly are two approaches that you should take simultaneously:

- The first is to work hard at any opportunity that comes your way, and to use the best talents that have been bestowed on you by your ancestors and your God. Through your parents, relatives and neighbours you would have acquired knowledge and skills in certain areas. Quite often you find yourself pulled towards the kinds of things that your family has become famous or renowned for. Now your family and your ancestors are always delighted to see you follow within the tradition they left behind and passed on to you. Your desire and their desire, of course, is that you use this opportunity to excel beyond what your parents and ancestors were able to accomplish.

- The second approach is to actively discover other talents that you may have, that you have not yet fully discovered. The idea is to eventually discover that thing that you are most passionate about. In life you will achieve more than most if you have the privilege to discover your real passion, when you still have enough time and energy to pursue this interest. It is quite easy to know if and when you are passionate about a career or preoccupation. When you discover your passion and you are engaged in it, time comes to a standstill. You love this preoccupation so much, that suddenly you discover boundless energy inside yourself, in order to pursue it. The end result is that you achieve a lot, and at the same time really enjoy yourself!

But remember, you can only discover your interest and passion by *taking action*, by doing things. As I have said, this interest and passion may be related to the fields or skills that your family has given you direction to, or it may be things that are new within your family, but for which you are discovering new energy and passion.

As you move along in life, it is important that at every moment in your life you do establish the major purpose of your existence at *that point in time*.

The fact that your purpose in life may change as time goes on, is not important. As long as at each moment you are leading a purposeful life.

I learnt this from a young age, because my mother is a hardworking taskmaster. Like most young people, I used to think that if I can finish my work, then I can relax and that if I cannot think of any more work to do,

I do not have to work. But every time my mother caught me not occupied with anything, and I gave her the excuse that there is nothing to do, or that I just finished the task she set me, then I got the biggest lecture of my life: "You always have to find something to do for yourself, something that is worthwhile at any point in your life."

This is the spirit that prepares you for great things in life. It is the same spirit that allows you to stumble on ideas and opportunities which otherwise are hidden. Some people think that luck happens by pure chance. My own experience is that luck is the result of hard work, thinking ahead and generally being prepared to identify an opportunity when it occurs.

Those who have led a purposeful life and work hard and are prepared are more likely to see an opportunity when it arises. When such people succeed, or achieve great things, the lazy ones are likely to think that you are just lucky. The truth, however, is that luck is a combination of preparedness and making use of opportunities that come your way.

Chapter 7
Manage your Attitude

The Third Pathway:
Iva munhu anozvibata

**Hold yourself with a long heart
and happiness all the time - manage your
emotions to keep a positive attitude!**

First, be a happy person, no matter what. Afrikan wisdom says that you must first be a happy person, before you can achieve great things in life. In today's world, we are obsessed with achieving material goals, as if to say that we do not get a licence to be happy, until we have achieved something physically. This explains why so many 'successful' people are depressed people. Most so-called successful people tend to be driven by the need to achieve certain material goals. Quite often, they are determined not to be happy until they achieve their goals.

In today's world, where so many middle-class Afrikans seem to be confused about life in general, you find that most actually believe that happiness is a direct result of achieving certain material goals. The problem is that, even though achieving material goals is a worthy activity, if this is pursued in a manner that disregards maintaining good, worthy relationships, with your self, spouse, family members, relatives, friends, quite often by the time you achieve the material goal, you have lost a lot of connectedness that is important to achieving true fulfilment in life! As a result, often we have people who have achieved material success in their careers and business, but at the same time they are people who have lost their capacity to relate to others and therefore are often not able to achieve real happiness in life. Sometimes this even pushes them towards trying to achieve higher material goals, hoping that this brings them happiness. But tragically, this only fuels jealousy and greed.

As a young professional, well educated and well trained, I really looked forward to my first job. And I always imagined that I would work hard and buy myself a very nice car. In fact, I was determined to buy a fancy German car and determined not to be happy until I bought myself that car. But then I realised that the harder I worked, without paying attention to my emotional and spiritual growth, the more meaningless it became whether I achieved all my material goals.

So by the time I bought myself a nice BMW I already knew that that was not going to be the source of my happiness. In fact, it should not matter at all whether I failed buying the BMW or ended up buying a cheaper car. The sad part for me is that I see every day in middle class Afrikans, my relatives and friends, my children, my brothers and sisters and cousins, that the pursuit of happiness is very elusive. Most find themselves either divorced, or disconnected with friends and people who mattered to them in life, well before they achieve their material goals. And this should not be the case.

Achieving worthy goals, materially, is good, as long as it is not a condition for happiness. In fact, I would go as far as saying that those people who are good happy people, with a 'long heart' first, before they become wealthy, will find themselves happier as they achieve greater success in life. And quite often, these are the people that use their greater success to the greater benefit of society and humankind.

In life therefore, it is important to tell yourself every day: "I will be a happy person and infect other humans with my happiness, all the time!"

Afrikan wisdom says that wealth is good and important in eradicating poverty and the physical hardships of life. It is not acceptable, however, in an Afrikan sense, that wealth is created in its own right, without a greater goal or worthiness for society. In fact, Afrikans have a lot of respect for people who achieve success and wealth through hard work and provision of goods and services that are of greater value to society. However, according to historical wisdom, Afrikans have always been highly suspicious of unexplained wealth or instant wealth, particularly the kind of wealth that does not emanate from worthy service and products to society at large.

Of course, as I achieve worthy goals in life, it will enhance my happiness. But when I meet obstacles and hurdles, I still want to remain a happy person.

To be a generally happy person, you need a 'long heart' or 'moyo murefu' in Shona. And a long heart, in Shona, means acceptance, patience, and tolerance, as well as unconditional love for yourself and for others. 'To hold yourself' or 'kuzvibata'-basically means to manage your own emotions. Our ancestors discovered emotional intelligence well before Western scientists gave it a name. But in order to manage your own emotions, so that they work better for you, you need to understand yourself and know yourself.

So the first step in achieving a 'long heart' is to know your true self. This is the basis on which you learn how to manage relationships with other people. To be human is the ability to manage your own emotions, so that in turn you can manage relationships with other people.

We have become far too used to blaming other people for how we act, and how we feel. This is wrong. Afrikan wisdom says that it is not what somebody says to you, or what somebody does to you, that ultimately determines what you do. Rather, it is the decision that you make for yourself about what you want to do, after somebody either tries to please you or to anger you.

If you have learnt to 'hold a long heart', you will be able to control your ego and your emotions, so that your behaviour is consistent with who you are, rather than who it is you are interacting with!

My experience of growing up in a big family with four brothers and four sisters, was that if you could get away with it, you could cause trouble and always blame it on some other child. We sometimes did this just by way of playing games. The sad thing is, however, that I have found that most people do not grow out of this behaviour to take full responsibility for their actions, even after they have become seasoned career people. Often people are not able to manage their emotions or attitude. As a result they blame others for how they think and feel, rather than accepting their ownership of those feelings.

In my young adult age I loved to drive, but I was also a very impatient road user. So of course, I was a cause of road rage, as well as being on the receiving end of it, quite often. But as I learnt to understand myself better and learnt how to manage myself the way I know my parents and those before them used to manage themselves, I realised that I really do not have an excuse for getting upset on the road, just because someone made a mistake in front of me. There was no reason for me to lose my temper just because somebody was deliberately trying to make me angry through the way they were driving. The bottom line is, the decision is still mine: whether to be angry or not!

Over time I realised that much more often than before, I could actually choose not to be provoked when I was being provoked. My feeling or reaction is still my choice. Quite often I have chosen not to be provoked, only to find that those trying to provoke me, get upset at the fact that I am not getting provoked! This means that it was their intention in the first place to upset me. But by simply choosing in my own time and space what reaction to have, I kept control of the situation and did not let myself be emotionally controlled by another person.

A 'long heart', therefore, is the most important internal form of control - it is your emotional 'on/off button'. The last thing that you want in life, is to have an external point of control, where your reactions and behaviours are controlled by other people.

This is very important to remember! In our times, the mass media like radio, television, newspapers or magazines often seem to control what people think and do. Do not let the media control you: always be alert to the messages that are sent out through the media and decide for yourself how to think or react about what you are seeing or hearing. In particular, remember that the media is an instrument used by those people who want you to 'buy in' to their ideas, vote for their political parties or buy whatever they are selling. In doing so, they will not shy away from using every trick in the book to get control over your mind or your emotions.

For instance, they will catch you when you are relaxing in front of the television set and your mind is not alert, by showing an advertisement that has a very sexy guy or girl using a product they want to sell. They combine this with cool American music and you get hooked! If you are not in control of your mind, you will not even notice that you are being made to believe that if you buy that product, you will either be as sexy as the guy or girl in the advertisement, or get a sexy boyfriend or girlfriend, like the one in the advertisement. On top of that, you will start believing that you need to act like an American if you want to be cool.

Appealing to your sexuality (using 'sex appeal') is the easiest way for anyone using the media to exert external control over your mind. If we are not aware of this, we easily fall into the trap of letting our basic instincts blur our brains into allowing us to do things that we should not do. This is one of the main reasons why people are overspending, overeating and obsessed with sex. But if you hold yourself with a long heart, there is no risk of 'losing control' over your own mind, emotions or body.

Always remember that a long heart is the closest thing to your true self and your spirit. It is the opposite of your ego. Your ego is your external point of control, because it is basically an inflated view of yourself, as you would like other people to see you. So obviously, if someone pokes at your ego, if your ego is too big, you are bound to react and get upset in an attempt to protect your image like you see it through your ego.

So your ego is not your true self. In fact, your ego is no other than an arrogant view of yourself. And arrogance and ignorance are very close relatives.

It is important to build your personal self on a day-to-day basis. Most people tend to assume that your habits and your character, are fixed and given and cannot improve over time. This is not true. In fact, you have to remind yourself each time you get up every morning, that you are going to do your best today and every moment of your life, in order to improve yourself to build your character.

You need to keep in your head a strong image of the kind of person you really want to be, so that when you go to bed every night and when you get up in the morning every day, when you take a moment of reflection every day, you have to remind yourself of the kind of person you really want to be or you are striving to be and the kind of things you need to do to improve yourself into that person.

The kind of person you are is made up of four major parts:

- your body
- your mind
- your emotions and
- your spirit

Let me explain a bit more in depth the importance of growing yourself and rebuilding yourself in those four parts. Your body is simply a physical expression of your being. Your mind basically encompasses the functional part of your person and ego. Your emotions help to connect you to other people. And your spirit is your true self that connects you to God.

Each of these four parts requires improvement, continuous improvement on a daily basis. Your body through eating the right foods and exercising, your mind through analytical thinking and creating knowledge, your emotions by managing them and choosing a positive attitude to life, and your spirit through strengthening your connectedness and one-ness with other people, nature, and God.

Remember, always hold yourself and manage your emotions so that they are appropriate to any situation that you are in. Have a long heart, so that you are able to be in charge of your emotions and all the decisions that you make for yourself. Lastly, be a happy person, unconditionally. First be happy, and then lead your life.

Do not wait until you land the big job, or make a lot of money, hoping that you achieve happiness afterwards. It simply will not happen.

First be happy, and then go ahead and conquer the world. In that way, you will always be happy, no matter what happens.

Chapter 8

Invest your Passion

The Fourth Pathway:
Ita basa nemoyo wako wose

**Whatever you do, do it wholeheartedly, with
all your strength and courage. This is the only
way to build a real world.**

There is no greater sense of fulfilment in life than
taking action and fulfilling a goal or purpose.
Working and acting out one's intentions and desires
is the most important thing towards reaching important
achievements in life. There is a Shona saying: '*kufuma
ishungu*', meaning 'true wealth lies in passion'. So it is
important in life to do your work wholeheartedly, with
all your energy and passion.

It is also Afrikan Shona wisdom that '*sango rinopa
waneta*' loosely translated as 'the forests will only give
you (food and clothes) when you are tired'. This means
that you need to work so hard yourself, that you do not

leave your ancestors any excuse not to reward you for your hard work!

Life is a journey and not a destination. Another way of saying this is, what is important in life is not what you have or what you achieve, but rather how you achieve it. Life is about the 'how' not the 'what'.

Our ancestors always knew that if we are just being blessed and showered with all the wealth in the world without any work behind it, this is hardly going to result in greatness and happiness. So, hard work and purposeful action is important in its own right. Action, however, only has meaning when you have clear intention. After all, you have to focus on the work and give each activity focus and attention if you want to achieve great results.

Nothing in life grows or flourishes if it does not get attention. And if you look around yourself, if you look at your home, your children, your relationships, your flower garden, the state of your house, your financial matters you, will notice quickly that only those things that get your attention are flourishing.

It is Shona Afrikan wisdom that '*basa mangwanani*', directly translated as 'work is morning'. This means that if you are serious about achieving something, get up early in the morning and get going. That is the only way that you apply your best energy and your clearest mind to your purpose.

This brings us to the fact that it is really important for you to understand your energy cycle and how nature works in your favour. Organise your work in such a way so that the most important things are done when you have the most abundant energy and time.

Also, you need to learn to organise your work in such a way that most of the things that you do are related in your mind. It is important to realise that most things in life are inter-related. No matter how distant physically or conceptually: most things are connected. So if you have multiple goals, multiple tasks to perform, it is difficult to achieve most of these if they compete for your time and attention. Some things will simply wither away and die from lack of attention.

So the way to manage multiple goals and activities is to sit down and rack your brain until you find connections between those important things that matter in your life. By being able to show and understand how separate things in your life that are important are related, it makes it possible for you to work on several tasks at the same time, with greater synergy between the different activities.

For example, like my mother and father, I am also the kind of person that tends to do too many things at the same time. I also want to do well in most of them. I have been fortunate in that I have done quite well in a lot of the things that are important in my life, such as my career, my family, my possessions, my relationships with friends and other loved ones, and so on. Even at work I generally tend to work on a large portfolio of activities. Maybe people wonder where I get all the energy and time to do all this work and still achieve good results in most of them.

The answer is very simple: all the things that matter in my life are completely inter-related in my mind. I search and look for the connections and grow those connections all the time, so that the moment I am working on the most important thing at that time, I am automatically working at all the other things, even if slowly. By working on the one thing, I am adding to all the other things.

Once again, this is not a product of logic or intelligence, because I am no more intelligent than most people I know. But instead of using only my own intelligence, I also use nature's intelligence. Nature automatically has most of the inter-connections that we are looking for in life. By carefully studying nature you find that you can learn a lot about inter-connectedness.

It is also Shona Afrikan wisdom that *'chawawana batisa, midzimu hayipi kaviri*, meaning 'Whatever you have achieved, hold on to tightly. The ancestors will not give you the same thing twice.' In the English language there is a saying that basically has a similar meaning, namely that 'a bird in the hand is worth two in the bush.' What this means is that it is worth investing more in whatever you have in terms of talents, whatever you have already achieved in your business or career, or an existing relationship, rather than trying to invest your attention elsewhere. So hard work on and attention to what you already have is more likely to open up other connections to related activities and opportunities, instead of trying to increase your portfolio of work and activities. Investing your time and attention in business opportunities and a career that are related or that enhance existing relationships, will allow you to achieve more and more in life with less and less effort.

Chapter 9

Give Generously, Receive with Gratitude

The Fifth Pathway:
Batsira vamwe.

Help others, give to others, receive from others and be thankful in giving and receiving from others.

There is no greater gift you can give to another human being than to provide support and help.

Being helpful to your family, spouse, friends and workmates is the one thing that builds strong relationships.

It is important for you to enter any form of relationship or partnership with an attitude that says "I am going to be as helpful as I can". You do not have to be an expert, you do not have to be wealthy, you do not have to be physically strong, yet you can be the most helpful person in any relationship or situation. So, to be helpful is an attitude.

One can be helpful in all sorts of ways. And one can give in many different ways. I know that in today's world most Afrikans have lost the traditional Afrikan wisdom, which basically says that giving and helping is beautiful, particularly when you give and help in non-material things.

Most Afrikans today think that money is the most important form of giving or the most important gift to receive. And a lot of young Afrikans flock to churches and other private organisations pledging and offering money, believing that that is the most important form of giving and helping, while this is not the case in real life.

Often Afrikans today are more likely to be unhelpful at home towards family members, relatives and friends or work colleagues and then instead go to give a lot at church or a society.

There is this mistaken belief that this is what God wants and this is what is best for people in a modern world. But certainly, that is not true. You have to help, support and give starting with your family, relatives and friends, because physically and spiritually those are the most important people in your life. It is also important to realise that in Afrikan culture and wisdom, receiving is just as important as giving. In most relationships it is important and healthier that you give and also receive from those who mean a lot to you. In fact, in some instances, receiving is far more important than giving. Once again, Afrikans are losing this basic wisdom from our ancestors.

Let me give you an example: if you have a neighbour who is generally not as wealthy as you are materially, then the chances are that you are better capable of giving to them, than they are capable of giving new material things. However, you will find that, your poorer neighbour if they are true Afrikans, are more likely to give to you whatever they have or are capable of giving you as gifts, in the true spirit that you mean a lot to them. In that case it is important for you to receive their gifts with grace and gratitude, even if you may think that you don't need those gifts materially. You will find that if you just give and do not receive that relationship ultimately will not mean much to both parties.

In the true Afrikan spirit giving and receiving would take all forms and shapes. Helping and giving should not be restricted to material things. Of greater value than material giving is the giving of personal non-material gifts, and help. This includes giving such things as a warm greeting, thanks, appreciation, even through listening and giving attention to somebody is an extremely fulfilling form of giving.

In the same way, you should be willing to receive similar gifts from family, friends and relatives, because you mean a lot to them.

In modern day Afrika a very important form of giving and helping is the sharing of knowledge, information and skills necessary to thrive in today's tough work and business environment. So if you know something, or have just acquired a new skill or you find someone needs a similar skill, then teach somebody else. If each one of us gave ourselves the responsibility to teach somebody else something all the time, and that we ask somebody to teach us something that they know better than we do, we would be doing a lot better in Afrika today!

Let me give you an example of how I experienced this in my own career. Almost every job that I have had, I have found that in general I end up sharing or teaching somebody else a skill that I know or have. However, I found that the older I have become, that there are a lot of younger people, in some cases people who do not hold high positions at work, or may not even be highly educated formally, and yet I always find that they have something that I can learn from them.

In fact, in supervising other people at work I have found that some of my most fulfilling relationships with people that I supervise is with those with whom I have made time to get them to teach me something that they know, but that I do not know yet. So at work, there is nothing more fulfilling than teaching the boss or supervisor something that she or he does not know. Or if you are a boss, always be sure that you make yourself available to learn something from the people that you supervise and thank them and acknowledge them for the value.

In life, you cannot give what you do not have. And in turn, you should never go around taking things that you do not need.

What this means in practical terms is that you do not even have to think twice, when you are trying to figure out what you have to give or help with in any situation. Just give what you have. Do not try to give things you do not have. That becomes meaningless, superficial and difficult and may get you into trouble - financially or otherwise!

Similarly, do not go around asking people for things or knowledge that you do not need, just to impress them. Only take or ask for things you genuinely need. That is the basis of fulfilling relationships.

Chapter 10
Love To Learn

The Sixth Pathway:
Iva nechidakwadakwa cheruzivo.

Develop an insatiable curiosity for knowledge in life.

It is a valuable part of Afrikan culture to respect and value knowledge, and in particular, wisdom. Because wisdom is acquired through repetitive experiences, which then allows one the competence to know and judge better ahead of time. Afrikans always place a high value on old age, because it comes with the wisdom of experience.

At the same time, Afrikans also value youth and creativity. In general, therefore, Afrikans tend to accord or associate wisdom with age on the one hand and youth with creativity, experimentation and action on the other.

This always formed a very important strategy in the way traditional families and villages functioned in Afrika. For instance, on issues requiring experience, wisdom and informed judgement, the older people in society tended to have more say. On the other hand, in times of new challenges and new crises, younger people have always been brought in because of their greater propensity for trying things out, as well as enthusiasm when faced with new ideas and challenges.

In general, however, it is age-old Afrikan wisdom, that learning never ends from the time when you are born, until the time when you die – each one of us is learning continuously.

That is why it is important that we as Afrikans rediscover this important heritage that we seem to have lost. We need to provide greater space and opportunity for children and younger people to grow their capacity to be curious and learn.

One of the problems we face in modern-day Afrika is that our traditional and indigenous knowledge has been relegated to an inferior position compared to Western forms of knowledge. There is a sense that it has lost its value and importance. Once again, because we have been so badly brainwashed over the last couple of centuries, both Afrikans and non-Afrikans tend to assume that if knowledge has not been written in a Western-style book, or if knowledge is not taught in a formal school, college or university, therefore it is not knowledge at all!

Even worse, there is an assumption that science is the only true process through which knowledge is acquired and made legitimate. Once again, the end result is that in a modern world, in a modern Afrika, most of the valuable knowledge that has been gathered and developed over centuries, is sitting there either forgotten or melting away, because it was and is knowledge that so far has never passed through Western-style institutions.

It is very sad that as a result much of the indigenous Afrikan knowledge has been lost for good! And that on a daily basis we continue to lose this knowledge and wisdom. Each day, some wise old lady or man dies. All the knowledge they had is gone and gone forever...

We Afrikans have done very poorly in capturing this knowledge, either through writing it down or through promoting an ongoing oral tradition, in order to ensure that it is available to future generations.

Learning and knowledge is critical in a modern-day Afrika. I will offer you the three levels of knowing and learning that are of critical importance in our Afrikan society.

The first level is our ability to learn from existing knowledge in order to solve known problems. What I mean is that there is a lot of proof to suggest that Afrikans have lost their capacity to solve problems, facing them today, using knowledge that we actually had already acquired in earlier years.

At this level it is important for you and me as Afrikans, to invest more time and energy in gathering knowledge, making it clearer, writing it down and sharing indigenous and local knowledge that could still go a long way in solving today's problems and conflicts in the family, in the community, at work, within political parties and in government on a day-to-day basis.

The second level is our ability to borrow knowledge from others, and to do so intelligently. Afrikan culture is a dynamic culture. In fact, it always has been a dynamic culture. Over the last hundred years or so, Afrikan culture has lost its dynamism because it was swept aside as being an inferior knowledge system. As a result it is not used in modern states and in the running of modern states. However, it is still used in a limited sense in rural and other urban settings, where Afrikans realise that it is the only source of knowledge that they have in order to be able to function.

This all means that our capacity to borrow knowledge from others intelligently has been greatly reduced. One needs to have confidence, self-belief, and a dynamic culture and society in order to selectively and intelligently borrow knowledge from elsewhere, then bring it home and make it suitable and relevant to one's people and society.

The third level is the capacity to individually and collectively change our minds on major issues in life. Like any other dynamic culture, Afrikans had a time-tested approach to drawing the conclusion that a situation has changed so much, that the knowledge or understanding of a situation needs adjustment, or a 'paradigm shift' - that is a completely different way to look at things. This approach was the *'dare'* or *'imbizo'* described earlier on in this book. These consultative processes are a thing of the past, in terms of really having deep discussions on major issues. As a result it seems that Afrikans have lost to some extent the capacity to quickly address new challenges such as HIV/Aids and the continuously changing world scene created through globalisation.

I would like to suggest that we rediscover the first level of learning, through the process of gathering and writing up Afrikan sources of knowledge, wisdom and stories, as well as folklore and have these available in local languages. It is through Afrikan stories, folklore, mythology, praise poetry, proverbs and so on that we find a wealth of Afrikan wisdom just waiting there to be tapped by all of us.

The sad part is that we are more likely today to repeat English and Chinese proverbs and wisdom, than that we are able to share the abandoned heritage of Afrikan wisdom that is more relevant to our situation.

Our ancestors also knew very well that nature is the greatest teacher of all and that we learn so much for free from other animals, birds, trees, mountains, rivers and other living plants and organisms. I will talk more about this in the next chapter.

In today's globalising world, knowledge is really the most valuable thing anyone can have. Knowledge is also becoming the most advanced form of power. One could say that, if you look at power in general there are probably four major sources of power and one suppressed form of power in the world today.

The first of the major forms of power is violence. In fact it is sad to say that violence is probably still the single most significant form of power today. It is sad, because it just goes to confirm that we think we are human beings, but in reality most nations are being led by people that have become sub-human, because they ultimately exercise power over their own people and other peoples using violence as the major force.

The same applies to family and community level. Because of the decay in Afrika that we have already talked about, we find that once again violence is emerging as the most significant source of power in the household and community, mostly leading to the abuse of women and young people. This is a symptom of modern-day Afrika and does not in any way represent Afrikan ancient wisdom. My evidence for this is very simple: once again, if our ancestors were able to craft a system where no-one young or old, male or female, goes destitute, if our ancestors crafted a family and extended family system that is the best social security system in the world, it follows therefore that it could not have been put together through violence as the major force.

In fact, the only way in which this incredible system could have been built, is if love was the major force – an unconditional love for relatives.

The second force that is strongly used in the world today is organised ideology. This is largely expressed through politics and religion. Both use mass cohesion and peer pressure and often manipulate people through social mobilisation. Sadly, political power is often used as a kind of legal form of violence. The reason for this is that once someone gets political power, it can be used to turn national forces of protection, such as the police, army and intelligence services into national forces of violence.

The third force of power in the world today is money. Money can be used to buy both political and religious support, thereby giving even greater access to means of violence and control. If used wisely, however, money can be invested for greater peace and progress of a people.

The fourth source of power is knowledge: together with love, the fifth force, knowledge is a source of power that is spiritually-based. Also, like love, knowledge is a source of power that can be shared without diluting it. In fact, when knowledge is shared, it still remains with the giver. This means that knowledge - similar to love - can grow through sharing.

With the other three forces, the power is diluted the moment you share it. This applies to violence, ideological or religious power, or money. Which means that those three are an inferior source of power.

So if you and I are going to be agents of change in the world today, if you and I are going to change Afrika for the better, the greatest investment we have to make is in knowledge. And the most important of all that knowledge is *Afrikan* knowledge and wisdom, as well as knowledge and skills to create more local, indigenous, Afrikan knowledge for a modern, globalising Afrika.

I believe, like most of my fellow Afrikans, that Afrikan knowledge is an incredibly valuable form of knowledge. It is as good as any other knowledge created by another culture. Because in certain respects it would be different to other forms of knowledge in the world, and can offer better answers to some of the questions that other cultures have, it is our duty to share the best of the knowledge we have in Afrika with the rest of the world.

It may actually turn out that, the knowledge that the world is missing today, in order to be a more peaceful and healthy world, is the kind of knowledge that we have in Afrika. As I've said earlier, the Western world is very advanced in technological knowledge and we as Afrikans are unlikely to out-compete them in the medium term. I also suggested that the Eastern world is far too advanced for us to beat them in the medium-term, when it comes to process engineering and manufacturing. I also say that, however, when it comes to knowledge about people and relationships, and if we are talking about knowledge around being human, then we Afrikans are very advanced and have a lot to share with the rest of the world.

I know that it may sound a little far-fetched to you, but I honestly believe that, if this Afrikan knowledge - people-centred knowledge - could be grasped by the East and West, this would combine worldly or materialistic knowledge into a more progressive force that would be more likely to create the kind of international environment for broader peace, prosperity and the freedoms of people. It is through knowledge and love that the final frontier of human 'one-ness' is going to be achieved. This is a necessary step in the long-term process of uniting all the peoples of the world, as well as harmonising all of God's creations. As that happens, political boundaries will become meaningless. And as that happens, God's original intention of one people, who are at one with nature, will be achieved.

Chapter 11

Celebrate & Respect God's Creations

The Seventh Pathway:
Yemura, zvisikwa zvose zvamwari; zvose zvinoera □
Celebrate nature and all of Gods creation's □ *all God's creations are sacred.*

**All God's creations are sacred.
Celebrate, respect and appreciate nature and all of God's creations.**

Our ancestors were, once again, more enlightened than we are. They knew, without science, that nature is closely related to humans. Through DNA technology today we now know that Afrikans were always right. For instance, the DNA of a chimpanzee is 98% that of a human. That means, that we are 98% related to the chimpanzee in terms of all the ingredients that nature put into creating the two species.

For all practical purposes, we are cousins. DNA technology is also showing us today that, in fact, all mammals – elephants, lions, hyenas, and so on –all hold more than 90% of the same DNA as found in a human being. In short, while modern science is only able to prove this now, Afrikans have always known that we are closely related to animals, plants and water. Evidence of this knowledge is found in Afrikan stories and mythology. In Afrikan mythology there is no separation between animals and people. In fact, in Afrikan mythology animals can house a human spirit, and *vice versa*: a human can host an animal spirit.

It is not surprising therefore, that the bulk of the totems and clan names in Afrika, are based on animals. In Afrikan folklore humans, trees and animals are also much more closely inter-related. I remember as a youngster that I had the opportunity to listen to a lot of folklore stories from my grandmothers and other elders. It was quite amusing to find that in these stories, animal and people are speaking the same language and facing the same challenges. I remember at least one story, where a woman was married to a hare. I remember another story, where a woman was having an affair with the crocodile. And the poor husband who was initially very impressed about the wife's ability to bring home a lot of fish every day, was later on shocked to discover that she was madly in love with a crocodile and that this crocodile was diligently fishing fish for his lover!

I also remember many stories around how we humans have a lot to learn from animals. And this would cover all spheres of life, from power, politics, human relations, but above all about character and behaviour. One of my fondest set of stories was about the hare and the baboon. In Afrikan folklore the hare stands for a cunningly clever person. And the baboon really represents a dumb individual, who, however, is a very loving person. In the Shona version of these stories, the Baboon is the uncle of the hare. And according to Afrikan tradition the strongest loving relationship is between a child and his or her mother's brother. So in Shona tradition the 'uncle' is the mother's brother, not the father's brother. In any case, the hare is always making fun with Uncle Baboon, playing all sorts of practical tricks on him, but poor Baboon loves his nephew so much that, in spite of being embarrassed all the time, he still continues to love him wholeheartedly and unconditionally.

This of course means that there is an endless list of stories, where poor Uncle Baboon is embarrassed all the time, but still manages to embrace his nephew, the hare. But then you find that the hare, because of his tricky character, often finds himself in trouble and as a result has to be rescued by Uncle Baboon. This is an example of character-building folklore stories, that used to build youngsters in terms of behaviour formation.

I also remember how in Shona folklore the owl and the hyena are associated with witches. The owl is a night-bird, sleeps all day and is active all night. So the conclusion was drawn that the owl must be a witch. And because a hyena has shorter hind legs and likes to hunt at night, the myth developed that the hyena provides some means of transportation for the witch at night. In Shona folklore – as in many other Afrikan traditions - the witch is always riding on the hyena, instead of on a broom as in Europe. Isn't it interesting that, even in folklore, our mythology is more practical than European mythology?

Then the witch needs to see at night, which is rather difficult for human eyes, so the witch hires an owl and the owl has to sit on the shoulder of the witch as she is riding, to show the witch the way. Every witch in Afrika has an owl accompanying her.

You can imagine that I grew up not wanting to have anything to do with hyenas and owls! However, I'm glad to learn today through DNA-based science that I am much more closely related to the hyena than I ever thought.

The important message throughout is that in our relationship with nature and animals, we are all closely related and all part of one universe and directly connected to God and that, therefore all of God's creation needs to be regarded with utmost respect: it is part of us and we are part of nature.

The fact that these animals, trees and plants do not speak the language we speak, does not change the fact that they are all endowed with great knowledge and wisdom. You just have to watch a plant grow over time and over the seasons, to realise that it is only capable of doing so, because over the centuries that plant has mastered the knowledge and skill to survive, to reproduce itself, and to grow and flourish without much visible effort.

So in some sense the trees and the grasses are more intelligent than we are. After all, it takes a human being years and years to be able to survive without maternal and paternal support. And yet a lot of plants and animals have had to develop the internal intelligence to be able to survive from the onset without much help from anybody else. So seed or young baby plants have the ability to survive and hide and fight off potential enemies, germinate, grow, survive on very little, on whatever there is, and they do so without the screaming and shouting, that we humans seem to have to do to get some attention!

Afrikan wisdom tells us that all God's creations are intelligent and therefore are sacred. This means that as humans, with our greater capacity for violence, we should treat all God's creations as sacred. Our ancestors always knew that we should therefore always live side by side with animals and plants, and not hide them away in game reserves and fence them off, so that only the privileged few can see them. They always knew that life was about co-existence with animals, trees and rivers.

Our ancestors were quite clear about the fact that you only harm or kill another animal or plant for a worthy purpose. So when our ancestors used to go hunting, they would prepare and talk to the ancestors and God and when they get to the forest, they would once again speak to the local spirits and ancestors looking after that forest on behalf of God, to ask for permission so that they would be allowed to hunt in order to feed their families. No other harming or hunting of animals, just for the sake of fun, was acceptable!

Today, Afrikans are losing the connection with nature and wild animals very fast. Sometimes I actually believe that part of the spiritual deprivation I see taking over Afrika is partly because Afrikans have lost almost all connectedness to nature. This may be similar for other cultures, who have become highly urbanised.

What our ancestors used to take for granted, can no longer be taken for granted today. They would take the time to sit under a tree and discuss and thrash out issues at leisure and at the same time they were enjoying one of the most important ways of connecting with nature. They would visit forests and mountains and not only connect with nature in that way, but they also knew that the same forests and mountains also contained other spirits, bigger than them, also connected to God, that they had to respect and talk to through their own ancestors. Today, more and more Afrikans live in brick and concrete homes, far away from nature. Most Afrikans are trying hard to flock to major urban centres, where they live mostly in squatter camps. Most of them have absolutely no connection with forests, mountains, water and all the sacred creations of God that make it easier for us to connect to God.

No wonder that you see what is happening in most of these urban societies: the human-ness of people has been heavily devalued. In these huge metropolitan centres in Afrika, such as Johannesburg, Lagos, Kinshasa and so on, nothing is sacred any more.

Human life is no longer as sacred as it used to be. So a petty thief would rather kill somebody just to get a little bit of money, because human life is no longer as sacred as it was in the past.

Well, our ancestors had left us with the wisdom that human life, as well as all other forms of life, are sacred. They also left us the wisdom that any form of political power, has to ultimately be sanctioned and governed through the sacredness of people's lives and their connection to God. Sadly, this wisdom seems to have been long forgotten.

It is very sad to see today that most ruling political parties in Afrika have lost the sacredness of people and nature in their forms of ruling and governance. Not much care is given to the extreme suffering of citizens and in some cases, governments are even prepared to violently repress and or kill their own people, just to stay in power. If we were to learn from nature today, and look at the animal kingdom, we would learn that our ancestors would not permit such killing.

I would like to suggest therefore, that as a modern-day Afrikan, you should develop a new relationship with nature. I don't care where you live, or what you believe in, I will simply suggest to you that it is healthy for your mind and soul to periodically reinvent your relationship with nature. At every opportunity, go and visit your tribal home. Go there and seek out the tribal and family leaders in your community. Learn from them about your family and your relationship with nature.

Go out and visit nature. Walk in the forests. If there are no more forests in your area, go and find them wherever they are. Look for a mountain and climb a mountain at least every year or two. But always remember that before you do all this and throw yourself into deep forests and mountains, that you have to show some respect. You always have to talk to your ancestors and God to guide you and talk to the forests and mountains and thank them for their oneness with and protection of you.

Walking in forests and along large expanses of water is an important way of connecting with your own spirit. It is through a close association with nature that you rediscover your spirit, knowing full well that all this is evidence of a greater Force out there, that is infinite more significant than you are as an individual.

I also suggest that, as an Afrikan, collect all the stories about the animal kingdom that have been told in your family and clan. Write them down, or get your children to write them down, get them to draw the pictures and tell the stories to other people and other children. Store them on the computer and share them on the Internet with other people and especially other Afrikans, to help them, too, to reconnect with our collective wealth. This is an important form of giving.

In summary, we are related to all animals and other creations of nature and God. In fact, we are close relatives. So in as much as we love our relatives, we have to love nature and respect it, as well as learn from it.

Chapter 12

Laugh, Play and have Fun

The Eighth Pathway:
Tandara nekuita mafaro nevamwe

Have fun and games with others from time to time. This is the way in which your body, mind and spirit come together. Fun and Games build your 'Unhu-Ubuntu-Botho' spirit.

Looking back at the traditional Afrikan village there was always ample time and space put aside for fun and games. Fun and games are important in building the complete human being.

In many instances, fun and games also offer ingenious ways of surfacing other serious issues in the community and sometimes providing a safer environment in which to discuss and share otherwise sensitive and contentious issues. It is important to ensure that you make time periodically to participate with others in the family and community in various fun games.

One of the things that I enjoy most is listening to and playing traditional music instruments and songs. The drum and the marimba are the most significant musical instruments in the Shona tradition. The spirit of Afrikan music has always been that everyone participates: the old, the young, male or female, it does not matter. In Afrika, everybody participates in song and dance. Traditionally, we don't just watch other people sing and dance, whilst we are seated. We all participate.

In fact, in Afrikan music, there is no music without dance. There is also no dance without the rhythm of music. Music and dance is not an academic exercise. We are all expected to participate fully. Some traditional instruments and songs are associated with certain rituals in society and the community. So there are special songs for weddings, for funerals, for worshipping God with the ancestors or for simply just having fun or celebrating.

In my part of the world, only the drum is used for religious ceremonies and the rituals to do with connecting with the ancestors and God. In another part of my country, it is the *marimba*, which is the ultimate musical instrument that draws ancestral spirits closer to the spirit medium, so that we can have a conversation with them.

Traditional songs, music and dance provide a greater sense of belonging and connectedness to your people and your history than simply confining your listening to contemporary music. In fact, it is important for you to emulate your traditional dances. After all, it is not important how good you are as a dancer, it is just well appreciated that you are participating at whatever level or skill and energy that you are capable of.

This all adds up to the spirit of togetherness and 'oneness'.

Part of having fun and games includes sharing stories, poking fun at each other, and all other forms of poking fun at oneself. It is extremely important for the soul and spirit that we are able to laugh at ourselves. It is equally important to be able to appreciate it and even have fun when others are poking fun at you! This is how our ancestors devised a way of ensuring that our egos don't grow so big that it becomes difficult to get advice or correction from others. My guess is that, in today's Afrika, most of our leaders have forgotten how to have fun and have also forgotten that it is important to periodically be embarrassed and deprecated as a means of having fun. Most Afrikan leaders, unlike is expected of Afrikan wisdom, have lost the capacity to laugh at themselves. As a result they have a limited amount of tolerance, and a limited capacity to listen to advice and criticism or simply listening to other, different voices to theirs.

In today's world it is generally hard to eke out a living. Most people are working long hours under stressful conditions. And quite often, professional people are finding it difficult to manage the stress levels that they generate at work. This inability to manage stress is a serious problem amongst Afrikan career people and professionals. Part of the problem is that historically stress was a Western disease. Traditionally, Afrikans did not experience stress the same way as people in the Western world experienced it. But you see we have been emulating the West so gingerly, that now the disease has caught up with us.

Stress is a silent killer. A lot of Afrikans suffer and die, before they even know that it was stress. It is a disease that we are not used to. We now need to address it headlong and rely on our Afrikan wisdom to deal with it.

First and foremost stress is a problem only when one is overwhelmed by work and expectations. Stress that is caused by temporary excitement is not necessarily bad. In fact, it may even be good if it stimulates you to jump into action and execute. Stress becomes a serious problem, when you are so overwhelmed that you keep pumping adrenalin and other juices in your system until they become poison. Each time that you pump this adrenalin in your system because you feel threatened and overwhelmed, the problem is that you need an effective way of eliminating all these toxins. If you were a wild animal, for instance, it wouldn't be a problem at all! Because then, if you were frightened, you would simply run away, like a zebra does, when it sees a lion. When a zebra sees a lion it produces adrenalin in the system, but then burns up the adrenalin immediately through the exercise it gets from running at top speed through the grass to get away from the lion. Sadly, running away is not acceptable human behaviour in the face of stress. But the funny thing is that zebra's have no stress levels at all, although they live side by side with lions, while we as professionals, living far away from the lions, suffer greater levels of stress, because once we pump adrenalin in the system, the system is getting ready to fight or run away. Most of the time in work situations, you neither run nor fight. You just sit there, until the next time you pump more poison in the system. That is why it is so important for us to find an outlet for our stress through creating opportunities for fun, games and physical exercise.

Let me give you a personal example. At the age of 33 I became the youngest Dean of a Faculty at the University of Zimbabwe. I was a very hard worker and supremely confident of my ability to execute this job, much better than my older colleagues. I worked so hard at making a success, I hardly noticed that my stress levels were going up. In fact, I didn't even really understand what people were talking about when they were talking about stress. I thought it is not possible for a rural, barefoot Afrikan boy like me to ever experience such a ridiculous problem. But the symptoms were there. I just didn't know that these were stress symptoms. My energy levels were lower. I would get up in the morning and instead of feeling fresh, sometimes I would get up tired. I didn't know it was stress, I just thought that I'd had a bad night. I also started realising that the joy of work was now receding. I wasn't enjoying my work as much as I used to. Even at times when I was achieving all my goals, the joy and excitement was gone! In fact, sometimes it made me feel worse, when I achieved something. I did not know that all this was due to stress. Not to mention that my temper deteriorated. My nerves were now so sharply wired because of stress, that it was not too difficult to upset me. And I am sure at times I was simply losing my cool with my children and spouse, because I had lost a level of tolerance owing to stress.

One day on a Saturday morning I got up and decided to have an easy day, because I had been too tired for some time. The surprising thing is that later on in that morning, when I was supposed to be relaxing, my heart started racing. I did not understand why this was happening to me. And each time my heart started racing again, I would feel this instinct to want to run away, or just run. I got scared and got someone else to drive me to the doctor. The doctor immediately strapped me on to the ECG heart machine and after doing all the readings, said to me, there was actually nothing physically wrong with me. He said that this was the result of the high stress level he had always warned me about and that I had chosen to ignore.

I did not believe what the doctor was telling me and I asked him to do more tests. I thought that maybe my digestive system was not functioning properly. So my doctor ordered all tests that were possible, including all sorts of blood tests. When the results came, everything was negative. My doctor sat me down and said to me, listen, son, I am seventy years old. I know that you are suffering from stress, you just don't want to believe it. My doctor then educated me on this problem and I also started educating myself.

It didn't take me long to start experiencing the benefits of good exercise, eating better food and having fun and games. But above all, I embarked on a process of managing my work and my priorities more carefully, so that I would have a more manageable portfolio of activities. This includes giving priority to the most important things in my life and ensuring that those are more closely related. Also, I started delegating a lot of other things that I know I can hand over to others without losing performance and control. But above all, this experience changed my life completely. It did not only remind me of my own limitations and mortality, but also allowed me to quickly rediscover myself as a less intense person and to develop myself into a much more relaxed, tolerant and fun-loving person. At that time at the young age of 33, I could hardly manage to walk up three flights of stairs without losing my breath. Twenty years later, at the age of 53 I can climb twenty flights of stairs without any difficulty and without losing my breath. So I am healthier at 53 than I was at 33, because now I understand the important of good health, fun and games.

So physical exercise is an important element in burning all the extra, unneeded adrenalin and energy in your system. Fun and games are a good solution to relieving stress levels. This is because you have an opportunity to burn all the toxins in your body. In addition, being absorbed mentally and physically in another activity, such as fun and games, also allows your mind to forget about the stressors in your life, thereby refreshing your mind and body at least until you face a stressful situation again.

In summary, therefore, fun and games are important for a healthy, body, mind, emotions and spirit. So go out there and play!

Chapter 13

Talk with and Listen to Others

The Ninth Pathway:
Gara dare nedzimhuri nevavakidzani

Regularly sit down and have consultative discussions with family, neighbours and relatives. This is the surest way to build functional relationships in life.

'Dare☐or 'consultative discussion' is one of the greatest inventions of our ancestors. There is no issue too great or too small not to warrant a round-table consultation and discussion. But this has to happen at all levels – at family level, to include the immediate family; at extended family level, to include the clan leadership and other involved parties, and at community level, particularly around local political issues.

The '*dare*' process in Shona culture, and a similar process in other Afrikan cultures, was a means of accomplishing so many aspects of village life. *Dare* was used at a higher level as a judiciary process, to resolve conflict. *Dare* was used for problem-solving meetings, where deep-level dialogue and brainstorming and problems are resolved. *Dare* is also the place for practical education and mentoring of younger people, as they get inducted into the issues of leadership and day-to-day living and management. *Dare* was the single most important instrument of teaching and actually living the philosophy of *Unhu-Ubuntu-Botho*.

I am disappointed to observe, however, that the *dare* process is slowly dying, particularly at family and extended family level. The quality of leadership at family and extended family level has been severely eroded in the last fifty years. Leaders of family and extended family, myself included, are not doing enough to convene and hold family meetings, including observation of family rituals and important occasions.

Family rituals are extremely important in Afrikan life. There is a wide range of important rituals in Afrikan family life, including marriage, death, and funerals, sorting out family inheritance issues, observing religious rituals to connect with departed ancestors and close relatives, as well as assisting in resolving challenges and conflicts within the family. More importantly, family gathering is where important plans and decisions are made, that are important for the progress of the whole family.

In spite of having one of the strongest family traditions in the world, Afrikans have sadly failed to date to convert this tradition to benefit them in terms of commerce and industry. Unlike Indians, Chinese and Jews, who have modernised their family system to take advantage of business opportunities, Afrikans have failed to use the family structure to good advantage in the business and commercial world. One has to look at a how different cultural groups or ethnic groups have organised themselves in exile or in diaspora. There is no question that the Chinese, Indians, Jews and other groups have done exceedingly well in using family networks to run global businesses from various capitals of the world. As a result, there is no major capital in the world, without a China-town or a strong Jewish community and they maintain their networks throughout the world, shuttle around, and moving family businesses. More importantly, these ethnic groups have mastered the art of supporting one another, allowing inexperienced family members to access experience and capital to eventually start their own businesses, thereby growing the wealth of the family as a whole.

We Afrikans on the other hand, have maintained strong family ties, but do not use them for business, if anything, for some unknown reason. When it comes to business, we shy away and avoid working with family members. Part of it is once again that we were brainwashed and in turn thoroughly brainwashed ourselves into believing that family businesses are inferior, and that in fact, employing relatives and friends in your business is morally wrong, usually referred to as nepotism.

In reality, the rest of the world has a majority of businesses run by family companies, where it is good practice to work with family members. The only place where employing family members above other people is inappropriate, is in public service positions. In business, working with family members can have great advantages.

Part of the colonial brainwashing was based on the fact that the new colonisers had to convince local people to work for them, rather than for themselves. But over time, the problem has been that because Afrikans were poorer and generally didn't own the larger manufacturing businesses, tended to equate urban-based jobs, working for a large company, superior to self-owned businesses. Furthermore, we modern Afrikans brainwashed ourselves into thinking that products and services supplied by big foreign businesses are of superior value to locally produced products. Quite often, we purchase inferior quality products, particularly food, simply because it is manufactured and packaged nicely, whilst at home we don't give much value to own traditional, healthier food and products that we should be producing and selling to our relatives, friends and the rest of the world.

Another problem is that at the time that most Afrikan governments attained independence, they became pre-occupied with the urban community, which tends to be more politically powerful, than the majority of people in the rural areas. As a result, most government policies favour urban labour and urban businesses. This includes such policies as cheap food for urban people, and therefore taxing rural people through poor prices for their agricultural products. It is sad to observe that in some countries, particularly in southern Afrika, where there is a limited number of small informal businesses, most people rush to expensive supermarkets and expensive stalls under the false illusion that they are getting a better quality and status product, than simply buying from their friends and relatives, who can produce a lot of products in a much cheaper and more accessible fashion. This includes such products as basic foods, grain, vegetables, dried fruit and vegetables, dried meats, cooking oil and so forth.

In summary, the inability or rather the fact that we modern Afrikans have depreciated our convening capacity of the family, and also lost the central essence of the family as an economic unit, means that we are less likely today to form strong family businesses and compete favourably with other nations with strong cottage industries, such as Italy and others.

Convening thc dare at family and community level is the surest way of building leadership capability within the family. It is also a way of building problem-solving capabilities within the family, as well as institutional memory. The dare is also a significant space for education, which is not normally available in the schooling system. This includes education on ones family history, ones culture, as well as the life skills and knowledge needed for survival in today's world.

It is at a *Dare* that I have developed experience in the art of problem-solving as well as conflict resolution. Traditionally, Afrikans acquired the skill of problem-solving and conflict resolution through acts of tolerance and compromise, as well as perseverance in seeking consensus. These qualities of tolerance and compromise in particular have over time been some of the most important ingredients in exercising judgment and in being a good human being. So this is central to the functioning of every community.

But even in political life the *Dare*, once again, is the most important instrument in participatory democracy. It is through the *Dare* that you as an individual can fully participate with family and other community members in being a citizen and exercising individual and collective responsibility for processes and decisions in your family and community. Without fulfilling your citizenry duty, it is difficult to have communities who are able to fully participate in national issues of politics, governance and the economy.

Dare is basically a traditional way of conducting round-table discussions. There are a few basic values and processes that make this unique institution as valid today as it was in ancient times. Firstly, to hold a successful *dare*, it is important for the leader of the family or the community, to invite and convene all the affected parties on the particular issue. This requirement that all affected parties are present, is so critical, that most *dares* don't proceed until the full membership is present.

In executing the *dare*, there are several processes, which have to be observed. The first is outlining the issue or issues on the table, one by one, and explaining them, as an initial start, so that everybody concerned is fully agreed as to what the issue is, and the kind of outcome that is required. In the Manyika (Manica) group of Shona-speaking people, this part is so important that they require everybody present to outline the issue and explain it one after the other, starting from the youngest to the oldest. The fact that the issue is repeated, in order from young to old, would normally be regarded as tedious in Western culture or even other ethnic groups in Afrika, but the Manyika Shona's have maintained this procedure to ensure that everyone present, and in particular, the young people, are forced to outline the issue and explain it in detail, so that they can own the issue and demonstrate the full understanding of the serious matter before them. It is only after everybody has agreed on the full significance of the issue and the outcome required, that the matter can proceed into fuller dialogue.

Depending on what the issue is, the matter is then dealt with. The main difference is whether it is a judicial issue, or simply a conflict resolution or dialogue issue. In case of a judicial issue the *Dare* is configured as a family or community court. The procedure then is such that the prosecutor or somebody representing the community, outlines the case before the defendant. And of course, the defendant is given his or her turn to offer their evidence before a full-scale discussion ensues.

At various points in the discussion, the leader of the family or village or chief, will guide the process to allow various contributions from various points of view, in some cases there would be a need for people who are experts in the area, to be given a chance to fully explain an issue or evidence. In some instances, you may simply have people who are respected in the community, as understanding such issues, to also weigh in with their experience, as the court seeks a just judgement on the issue. Almost always, the verdict is reached by consensus, before the head of the family, or community or chief, announces the decision and passes judgement.

In the case of conflict resolution or problem solving, or simply brainstorming and planning, the dare proceeds in a slightly different fashion and in a greater degree of brainstorming and cross-fertilisation of ideas.

In summary, different voices are given a chance to express themselves from their perspectives. Once again, some are considered experts on the issue, some are considered wise people because of their age and wisdom, some simply have an in-depth historical knowledge of the issue, and are therefore given a chance to speak. Quite often, it is not possible to have substantive data and information to always agree and resolve issues. However, there is always great desire on the part of a Dare, to apply principles of natural justice on an issue. This principle of natural justice may take various forms. For instance, if it is a legal or criminal issue, you may find that the lack of substantive burden of proof may not always discharge the accused. This is particularly the case if there is substantive displeasure expressed by major community representatives in the way that the accused generally discharges themselves in the community.

I know that in the Western world there is a preponderance of burden of proof, before people are found guilty, however, Afrikan heritage is such that we've always known that we don't have sufficient resources and technology to prove beyond reasonable doubt on every case. However, the historical record, as well as circumstantial evidence combined, can offer whole sufficient weight to punish defendants who are generally regarded as trouble-makers in the community or family.

I will give you an example of how my fathers and I used to handle cases of cattle theft in my village. If any of our family members lost their cattle, or believed that somebody stole them and we were not sure exactly who had done it, it often took one or two of my younger fathers to round the boys up, go and confront a few of those families, whom we know are reputed cattle thieves. The fact that my young brothers did not have enough evidence of who really stole them did not prevent them from threatening those families if we did not get our cattle back. Quite often the reputed cattle thieving families would take it on themselves to retrieve our cattle from their friends, who were also thieving cattle, and return them to us. In general, effective community processes are a much more cost-effective – in these cases it is quite acceptable to combine natural justice and burden of proof. This, of course, would not work in a Western world and will only work in Afrikan communities, where relationships and trust are very high – trust in the dare system and in these processes.

The whole essence of life is a search for peace, prosperity and freedom. We as Afrikans are today are the most troubled region in the world in terms of conflict or lack of peace, poverty or lack of prosperity, and human oppression or lack of freedom. This can all be traced back to our individual incapacity, as well as loss of value that Afrikans traditionally placed in playing strong citizenry roles at family and community level. I don't see how we can achieve peace, prosperity and freedom at national level, when we cannot achieve it at family and community level. I don't see how we can produce national leaders who truly understand the importance and value of peace, prosperity and freedom of people at community and family level, if these leaders never took responsibility to ensure that they succeeded in achieving these worthy goals at family and community level. Most of this leadership, like you and I, hardly fulfil the family and community responsibilities. Most of us are hardly able to lead a family or an extended family, like our forebears used to, so how can we expect then, suddenly, to be good leaders at a national level?

The English have a saying that "Charity begins at Home". In Afrikan wisdom you cannot succeed as mother or father of a nation, when you have failed to demonstrate capacity to lead a family or a community. But because of the over-confidence that our modern political systems are placing in politics through elections or in elections as being the most important instrument of democracy, what our political systems are producing throughout Afrika, are leaders capable of smooth talk and winning elections, rather than leaders born and bred as good human beings in a family, with the humility and tolerance needed for genuine servant leadership.

Chapter 14

Live according to the Unhu-Ubuntu-Botho spirit

The Tenth Pathway:
Tevera Unhu, ndiyo zhira huru yeupenyu

Follow the Unhu-Ubuntu-Botho spirit. This is the way of life, valued by your ancestors and that unites you with God.

Unhu-Ubuntu-Botho, or being human, is a way of life. For most Afrikan people and people of Afrikan origin *Unhu-Ubuntu-Botho* is a time-tested way of building yourself as a person and human being. *Unhu-Ubuntu-Botho* is also the time-tested way of building family and family processes. In fact, *Unhu-Ubuntu-Botho* is the only time-tested way of building communities and nations. Our ancestors crafted all the key institutions of *Unhu-Ubuntu-Botho* over a long period of time and used these processes to build the strongest family institutions in the world and with it, the least-cost social security system in the world.

In fact, colonialism and apartheid were only able to survive for so long, because of the great absorptive capacity of the *Unhu-Ubuntu-Botho* family system. *Unhu-Ubuntu-Botho*, therefore, is not only the way that our ancestors crafted for us, it is also the entry point and end point of all the various pathways leading to God.

By being a good human being and by embracing and leading your life through these pathways this is the time-tested way of thanking your ancestors and connecting with God. It is important to embrace these pathways as a way of life, rather than a religion. *Unhu-Ubuntu-Botho* never was an organised religion. In fact, religion was embedded in *Unhu-Ubuntu-Botho* simply as a neutral, doctrine-free way of making God and your ancestors part and parcel of your day to day life.

One of the growing misconceptions in Afrika is about 'ancestral worship' as a religion. As a matter of fact, this is another corruption of Afrikan culture and religion resulting from now more than a hundred years of colonial manipulation and misplaced values by modern Afrika. This is how it happened: our ancestors always knew that there is one God. They also knew that our ancestors are the direct connection with that God. Our ancestors devised a religion, which basically partners the living and the departed in communicating with God. This means that we don't worship our ancestors, instead we worship God. We simply just worship our God through our ancestors. In general, this means that

143

among the living, the most senior people in each family are the ones who will know and remember the recently departed. And because they remember them, because they lived with them and they name them it is easier to talk to them.

The idea is that we plead with them, to talk with the other departed, whom we as the living have never seen or interacted with, but we know that our recently departed are in direct contact with them. So the appeal is passed on from the recently departed all the way to the most historically departed that we can still name and remember through our oral tradition. Those are the ancestors that are finally able to pass on our plea and connect us to God.

Because this practice has been greatly disrupted and disturbed since the advent of Christianity and Islam in Afrika, much misunderstanding and confusion has come about. As a result, Afrikans over the years have become more and more confused as to how to connect with their ancestors and their God, as well as what role their ancestors play.

In some cases, some believe that you actually worship the ancestors. This is an error.

If you want a parallel with another religion, our ancestors play the same role as Jesus plays in Christianity – both are children of God and they are connected to God, so they can connect us.

However, there is a great tendency of living people to want to worship other individuals as Gods. This is the same error that is being made by Afrikans that worship ancestors, instead of appealing to ancestors to mediate with God on their behalf.

There are other Afrikans who are even more misguided. And these are the ones that go to traditional healers and actually believe that traditional healers can connect them to their ancestors and God. This is once again a corruption of Afrikan religion, simply because people are completely lost. If you want to connect with your ancestors you go to the senior elders in your family or clan. You do not go to non-relatives.

The reasons why some Afrikans go to traditional healers are of course similar to why people go to a Western-style doctor, namely because they are seeking worldly health and wellbeing. It so happens, however, that in most traditional medical practices, health and wellbeing is more holistic and embraces mind, body, cmotion and spirit to a much greater extent than does Western medicine. As a result many Afrikans who are suffering from various physical, as well as social stresses, end up seeking for spiritual advice from traditional healers for the same reason why other people would go to Western-trained psychologists. Quite often they end up getting the kind of counselling which tries to reconnect them with their ancestry or spirit world. This is not religion. This is merely seeking health and wellbeing in today's world. And this is not worshipping your God or ancestors.

In summary, therefore, Afrikans need to recognise this confusion and corruption that has spread in our culture. This is further reinforced by the negativity that is carried through Western-style education, media and, sadly, some religious broadcasts. In fact, I've witnessed how the Afrikan film industry is perpetuating some of these corrupt ideas.

For instance, when I watch a certain type of Nigerian film, I get so angry and embarrassed at how so many of these films are about witchcraft and some or other lower level spirit religion and how at some point in the film, some Christian entity comes in to provide a solution to a spiritual wilderness. To me this is shameful, that we Afrikans are perpetuating these corrupted ideas about our religion. It is just important for you to remember that religion is about God and not about a lower level spirit world. Spirituality is about connectedness with the world and God and that does not require a 'witchdoctor', or a traditional healer or a psychologist or a Western style psychic to make the connections for you.

You simply have to be. And the more you are simply relaxed in yourself, the more you are connected to your ancestors and your God. You don't have to be in a special room, you don't have to leave your house, you don't have to do anything. You are already connected.

Of course, now and again, you can join your family and relatives in religious rituals around your family, and ancestors and God. This is important for bonding and affirmation. However, it is not necessarily the only way that you connect with your ancestors and God.

One of the most serious damages to the Afrikan psyche is the separation of the Afrikan from our ancestors and God. The fact that historically our ancestors knew that their ancestors and their God are 'one' in that they are ever present, around and within every individual all the time, made religion in Afrika a practical proposition. This meant that every human being was a religious and spiritual individual. By removing religion from the day-to-day lives of people and making it an institution that expects one to go to church one day of the week and then forget religion for six days in a week, has made religion a very impractical proposition in the way it guides the day-to-day lives of people.

So, whilst most Afrikans dutifully follow the trend to join various churches and find peer acceptance in these modern-day social gatherings, this practice has not really contributed much to resolving Afrika's family, community and national problems and crises.

In summary, it is your responsibility as a modern Afrikan to look carefully at your life and belief system. It is important to reorganise your thoughts and actions so that you are once again able to fully know yourself and your family and the history of your people. It is important for you to remind yourself all the time of the transformative force that you are. And that the hidden potential in you can only be fully realised through rediscovering yourself as a proud Afrikan, proud in your culture, and proud in your heritage.

It is time to shed the baggage that you have been carrying for too long, that makes you think and feel that your culture and your language and your self are inferior to other cultures and languages. It is time to shed the inferiority complex, which emanates from the falsehood that foreigners know God or that their ancestors knew God more than your ancestors did.

The time has come for you to be completely proud of your ancestors, in what they did for you. After all, if it weren't for them, you would not be here.

Truth is relative. There is no such thing as absolute truth in the world. All truth is relative and personal. What you believe is your truth. And it is not possible or necessary to have universal truths, particularly on deep issues such as religion and culture. The most important thing is for you to appreciate and celebrate your culture and to connect to God, every day, and to do so through an understanding of a religion of your own choice. At the same time, appreciate, respect and enjoy other cultures. Exchange ideas and approaches, celebrate the diversity God created, and enrich your culture through this interaction.

So go forth as a happy, confident Afrikan. Go forth to revitalise yourself, your family and your community. Let us all do this, knowing fully well that we have to rebuild Afrika from the 'Foundation' and not from the 'Roof'. Let us realise that the nation-state in Afrika is a very weak and impractical notion. In fact, it is not desirable to have a strong state where we have weak families and communities, since all you have then is a benevolent dictatorship. Rather, let us rebuild our Afrikan society and see the great ascent of Afrikan peoples in the 21st Century as the direct result of modernising of our traditions and then borrowing intelligently from the rest of the world, as the only means of creating a great society.

We will never beat the Americans at being American. We will never excel over the Europeans at being European. We have absolutely no chance of exceeding Asians at being Asian. We, as Afrikans, however, will always excel over the rest of the world at being Afrikan.

So let's modernise Afrika, not Westernise it. Let's do so on the solid foundation of *Unhu-Ubuntu-Botho*, which our ancestors crafted over centuries painstakingly for us, because they love us.

Above all, the rest of the world is already looking to Afrika as the place from which the next great ideas about humanity are going to come from. The rest of the world has already exceeded at what they do best and they rapidly are reaching a point where they need help in the sphere in which they are the weakest in: and that is in building strong, loving families and inclusive communities, free of violence and drugs, and capable of combining peace, prosperity and freedom for all.

Afrika has to provide that missing piece for the rest of the world.

And this will start with you.

Chapter 15

Towards a truly Afrikan Renaissance

In this last chapter of my book on 'Being Afrikan', I want to introduce you to some of the thoughts that I have been having about rebuilding Afrika. I call this my 'General Theory'. Let me explain:

Afrikan society, like other societies, is made up of all three major spheres of life: social, economical and political. I recognised that Afrika has many problems in each of these three areas. As a result, I have developed a 'General Theory' over a period of time, because I felt that it is no longer possible to trigger a genuine Renaissance without crafting a general theory or idea that can explain why this decay in Afrikan society has happened on such a broad scale.

At the same time, I wanted to help provide overarching guidelines and answers as to how solutions could be holistic and be better placed to trigger mass progress. In other words, according to my point of view, trying to solve problems in Afrika on a piecemeal basis has failed to work. At the face of it an observer could simply say: "Oh, Afrika just has too many problems!"

My argument is that maybe Afrika just has *one* problem, which then manifests itself and triggers all the other problems!

In other words, my thinking is that by identifying the one central cause of the mass decay in Afrikan society over the last hundred years or so, we can also craft the basic principles and guidelines to make it much easier to enable a Renaissance.

Here is my 'General Theory' for the Renaissance of Afrikan society:

Historically, Afrikan society was built around family, extended family, neighbours, friends and the village community at local level. This is the place where citizens were formed. So all the key values of citizenry, of being a citizen, were developed at this level. This includes values around culture, economics and politics.

These three areas were the firm, irrevocable responsibility of the family and community-level institutions. Culture broadly included language, education, religion, holistic health and entertainment, while economics included food, shelter, exchange of goods and services and other business transactions. Politics and governance included the *'dare*☐ process, law, conflict resolution, and was basically trying to achieve peace, justice and equity.

Over the last hundred years or so and as a result of colonisation and Westernisation, these three areas of responsibility and accountability have slowly shifted from family and community towards the state, local government and non-governmental institutions. Meanwhile, the traditional institutions in Afrika were generally neglected and left to their own devices and as a result seem to die a slow and agonising death.

I believe that the decay in Afrika is the result of both incapacity of the Western style institutions, as well as the ongoing destruction of traditional institutions. Just look at the state instruments in any Afrikan country: none has real capacity to discharge full responsibility in those three important areas of society.

The end result is that at village level we have weak traditional institutions and processes, at the same time the local government system that most governments have put in place, has no real interface capacity with the traditional systems, which are still enjoying more respect within many especially rural communities. The end result is a worsening cultural decay, growing poverty, growing conflict, as well as an increasing incapacity to govern ourselves.

All these express themselves in various ways that are evident in any village life today, and this includes depreciation in self-esteem and self-confidence at individual and collective level, cultural disorientation, spiritual confusion, hunger and malnutrition, environmental degradation on a massive scale, family disunity and disintegration, dysfunctional political parties and government systems and growing violence, conflict and intolerance.

From my point of view, there are two main preconditions that need to be met before we can trigger a sustainable Afrikan Renaissance that will lead into the great ascend of Afrikan society. This includes, firstly, that we have to rebuild our own self-belief and self-confidence through a cultural revival and rejuvenation in all major spheres of culture and social integration. These areas include religion, language, education, music and art, amongst others.

Secondly, we have to restore the historical value placed on Afrikan knowledge and wisdom. Even more important is placing greater value on new knowledge created through social interaction and exchange, instead of placing so much value on reading books, written mostly in the Western hemisphere or by foreigners about Afrika. We have to shift the responsibility for education and learning processes back to family and community. It has not worked and will never suffice leaving the broad responsibility of education and culture to Western-style schools. We have to promote Afrikan ways of knowing and learning. Afrika has a highly-developed oral and visual tradition and we have to exploit the audio-visual media and methods such as roleplay more intensively for education and building of lifeskills, since these were the traditional means of conveying knowledge. Afrikans generally prefer to learn by doing, not by reading. Therefore, action learning and group interaction should be promoted as major pedagogical tools in schools and universities. Similarly, storytelling is an important tool in passing on Afrikan knowledge and wisdom. Stories are a more holistic way of combining knowledge, skills, wisdom and values in the process of educating ourselves. Isn't it interesting that 'telling stories' is suddenly becoming all the rage in modern businesses, as if this were a new, Western invention, while the value of storytelling as a means to share knowledge in a holistic way, as always formed the basis of indigenous education systems in Afrika? In addition, roleplaying, music, dance and theatre are extremely popular and participatory ways of learning and acquiring knowledge.

The problem today is that most Afrikans have been brainwashed to the point that we no longer believe in any other knowledge than that we read in books and newspapers. To make matters worse, if knowledge is not generated through Western-style processes, in particular if ideas and knowledge are not subjected to the rigours of the scientific method, then most Afrikan knowledge and wisdom is disregarded and generally relegated to myth, mysticism or insignificance.

So my 'General Theory' explains that the rebuilding of Afrikan society and the great ascend of Afrikans will need to be as follows:

Firstly, we have to rebuild Afrika from the foundation to the roof. At present, we have weak individuals, families and extended families and weak village communities. It is not possible to rebuild Afrika on this foundation. The current approach is of emphasising building the nation-state over a village community. This theory predicts that if we continue on this path, it means that we will continue struggling in this slow process of trying to build a Western-style nation-state, while slowly demolishing all the Afrikan heritage of values, wisdom and traditional institutions. The end result will be like a Western-style nation, which has a strong government, local government, business sector and civil society, but with tragically disintegrating families and village communities.

Secondly, we have to start the long-distance journey of individual and collective self-discovery once again, through culture, religion and so on.

Thirdly, we have to unpack and apply the ten *Unhu-Ubuntu-Botho* pathways at all levels of Afrikan life, from the individual, family, extended family, village community, local government, civil society, business and government.

Let us examine what this may involve by looking at each of the three major spheres of Afrikan society:

1. Culture

At present, Afrikan governments approach culture in the same way that Westerners approach archaeology, that is just revisiting the old traditions for curiosity's sake or historical knowledge and maybe for tourist and other romantic values.

This is not enough to contribute to an Afrikan Renaissance. You see, Afrikan culture may be sick (suppressed), but it is still very much alive and still provides the basic guidance for day-to-day living for most Afrikans on the continent. Cultural revival therefore, should not be for romantic purposes, instead it is about re-organizing and creating order in the day-to-day lives of people. And the start, once again, is the family and the village. Most Afrikan Governments tuck away culture in some corner somewhere where the focus is mainly on traditional dance and dress and the revival of some dying habits. This is sad. Governments must take a broader view of culture to include Afrikan languages, Afrikan religion, education from early childhood to tertiary level, traditional Afrikan science, art, music, theatre and all the things that make us Afrikans in terms of customary laws and leadership systems, and so on.

When it comes to the creative arts, music and dance, Afrika and Afrikans have a huge comparative advantage over many other cultures in the world. This should form a very strong pillar in how we craft and design the

Afrikan Renaissance. Of all global forces the creative arts and music are probably the most powerful cross-cultural means of relating and communicating. In the 21st Century it is clear to me that one universal aspiration of all peoples is the attainment of greater levels of human freedom and spiritual fulfilment. Creative art, music and dance have a major role to play in achieving this universal role. And Afrikans, with so much talent in these arts, can play a leading role globally in this regard.

However, although Afrikans are arguably the most talented creative force in the world today, this has not translated itself into prosperity for Afrikans. This has to change in all the spheres, including music, visual and performing art, fashion, theatre and other creative platforms.

This in itself will also boost our collective self-confidence as Afrikans. After all, the major source of all creative force can be traced back to the rich Afrikan heritage that we inherited from our ancestors.

2. Language and Education

Language is the single most important vehicle for cultural exchange and rejuvenation. Because culture is about the day-to-day lives of people, what we believe in, what we value, what acceptable ways of doing things are, it follows that education is an integral part of culture. In Afrika today, unfortunately, most governments treat education as something completely separate from culture. The end result is what we can see in Afrika today: widespread cultural disorientation, as people get more and more formally educated.

For an Afrikan Renaissance to take root, we have to aggressively and intelligently borrow technological knowledge from the East and the West. It is important, however, that all knowledge, local and foreign, has to be translated into local languages for the purpose of education.

I look forward to a slow, but steady process of ensuring that within a matter of a few decades, Afrikans will learn all levels of knowledge in their mother tongue. It is important for Afrikans, just like the Asians before us, and other European nations, that our children learn all knowledge, including mathematics, physics, biology and so on in our own mother tongue. Of course, we should still learn English, French, Mandarin and other foreign languages for purposes of business and cultural exchange with other great societies. But we should not use these as our primary languages for educating ourselves and our children!

Although it would appear that translating massive bodies of knowledge into local language is a mammoth task, difficult to achieve, I believe that this kind of task is increasingly more do-able, given the technologies that are currently being developed. I believe for instance that in another five to ten years we will have open-source software on the Internet, capable of language translation, at least for a few of the Afrikan language.

3. Spirituality

Afrikans are highly spiritual and religious people. It is important to rationalise how our traditional ancestor-based religion interfaces with organised foreign religions. Moving forward I would suggest that as a modern-day Afrikan we have to always remind ourselves that God did not give us this rare opportunity to have some time on this earth and then simply waste it away, trying to change or reinvent history.

Our ancestors and God wanted us here today so that we can create new history. So on religion, my primary message is about tolerance and inclusivity. Firstly, as an Afrikan it is important that you acknowledge and respect your ancestor-based religion. One of its primary values is that you have to respect all other religions. In other words, you don't have to convert other people into your own ancestral-based faith. And if an Afrikan chooses to pursue another faith, other Afrikans should not be intolerant of that choice. It is important that all groups in society keep their own faiths and beliefs. After all, we are all just trying to connect with God.

So it does not really matter to me, whether you are Christian, or Muslim, or Jewish, or an atheist for that matter. The important value to keep is that we are all equal in the eyes of God and we all have equal access to God through our own chosen means of faith.

The fact that through colonisation Christian missionaries made us Afrikans believe that worshipping through our ancestors is 'heathen' and therefore ungodly, and that instead there is only one way of connecting to God, should not translate into spiritual conflict in a modern-day Afrika. Instead, you have a responsibility to embrace and promote spiritual and religious diversity and ensure that no organised religion or faith dominates any other, either legally or implicitly, particularly in spheres of culture, education and politics.

For an Afrikan Renaissance, however, there are practical benefits that need to be restored in modernising ancestor-based religion. There are a number of practical losses we have suffered by shifting from ancestors to other intermediaries. One negative impact has been the devaluation of family as a form of identity as this shift occurs. In addition, love for family and relatives has diminished in favour of love for non-relatives. In general, there is more emphasis on "empathy" than there is on "love". This is why we now have so many destitute orphans today. In the past there was no choice because of love for family and one's "own blood". Today this is seen as a task for "do-gooders" who empathise or "feel sorry" for these unfortunate children.

In summary, spiritual revival, or re-kindling the dwindling love of other people especially your family and relatives, oneness with nature, and bringing back the sacredness of life in business, politics, and governance is essential for developing systems and institutions that promote peace, prosperity and freedom. By restoring sacredness of life in societal processes, people police and control themselves in the way they relate to each other, to nature and to other people's property. This is less costly way of developing an enlightened society without having to build huge police, military and judicial infrastructure to maintain law and order.

4. Politics and governance

Afrikans today are more confused than ever as to what constitutes legitimate leadership and governance systems at all levels of society. No wonder we are struggling to build legitimate and sustainable nation-states!

At the moment, the political party is the single most important organ in the shaping of a legitimate nation state. But the political party is another borrowed Western institution, just as we have borrowed the nation state concept. In this regard it is important for Afrikans to recognise that at this point in our history both the political party and the nation state are still largely irrelevant institutions to the general progress and wellbeing of people at the village and community level. In fact, the party political system is even facing major challenges in some of the Western world's important democracies.

The most important value of any political system is the capacity of people to govern themselves at all levels of society. As I have argued already, this has to start at the family, extended family and community level. It is important therefore that the political Renaissance in Afrika be informed first and foremost by how we see the rebirth of legitimate self-governance systems built around traditional leadership processes at the village level. And since even at village level people are not homogenous, but are part of different cultures, we as Afrikans have to find a way as to how to address this diversity, while still building on the useful values of traditional leadership processes and systems.

If people at the family or village level are not capable of governing themselves and are not capable of collective responsibility of mobilising resources around key needs and challenges, and if they are not capable of resolving most of the conflicts and challenges as they arise, using most of the available local capacity and resources, then we do not have a basis for building a legitimate nation-state or any other form of higher-level governance system.

The most urgent priority for any Afrikan head of state and government is to figure out what is really happening in your country at the family and village level in terms of political systems and governance. This is a prerequisite for any sustainable Afrikan Renaissance. Part of the problem today is that in every Afrikan country conflict continues to rage between the remnants of traditional leadership systems on one hand and the state-imposed local government system on the other. This has to be resolved as a matter of urgency.

The most serious challenge, however, is with political parties in Afrika. This is where most of the reform has to take place, if we are going to have governments and ruling parties that are able to sponsor and lead an Afrikan Renaissance.

Ruling and Opposition political parties in Afrika are a strange breed of institution, neither Western nor Afrikan. These parties generally rely on the worst of both Western and Afrikan political systems. From the Western political system, political parties in Afrika have generally adopted the 'winner-take-all' attitude, which comes with Western systems. That basically means that it is more important to win the election and then use that ticket as the basis on which to rule without meaningful consultation of the people being ruled!

From the Afrikan system political parties have wrongly borrowed the notion that leaders and the elders cannot be openly challenged or questioned on issues that affect the ordinary person.

My argument is that political parties in Afrika today are borrowing completely out of context and in a misguided manner from both Western and Afrikan political thought. A political renaissance in Afrika therefore requires us to borrow the best from the Afrikan and other political systems. In the medium term we are kind of stuck with the notion of a nation-state, which we adopted from our colonial masters and now religiously try and protect under some misguided notion of a need for nationalism. To make matters worse, governments hide behind the Western political notion of sovereignty to run away from all forms of accountability locally and internationally.

For instance no political party in Afrika should be considered legitimate if it does not adhere to the *Unhu-Ubuntu-Botho* principles of leadership and governance. In particular, political parties should be organised legally in a highly decentralised fashion, so that ordinary people in families and villages can exercise political choice and responsibility at the lowest stratum of society.

In fact, this raises the question as to why we even need political parties in the 21st Century? If we look at the recent elections in the United States of America and Germany, the lack of substantial differentiation in political thought between the parties has resulted in an embarrassing focus on trying to discredit the leaders of these parties through head-on character attacks, just in order to give voters some reason why they should vote for the one instead of the other! How can such a process be considered democratic – meaning 'for the people, by the people' - when even at the outset their leaders are seriously discredited? Surely, this approach must create a deep sense of unease about the ability of these leaders to run their countries effectively?

Starting from this basis, a political party or another form of civic participatory structure, should therefore follow the example of the '*dare*☐ process and be structured in such a way that the smallest levels of social organisations can see and express themselves in deed and practice in shaping the nation-building process, shaping the way government functions to meet their needs and generally to allow full ownership of their party or other form of civic participation and their government.

In addition, the processes of self-governance in the political party, should be based on *Unhu-Ubuntu-Botho* principles. This includes open dialogue, where consultation, deep dialogue, tolerance, consensus-building are the values that drive the political agenda. This is in major contrast to what I see today in most political parties, where leaders see their major function in 'talking down' to people all the time.

The same principles should apply to how the rest of the system of governance is structured in a country, from local government, parliament and central government.

It will continue to be an uphill battle in Afrika, to try to build legitimate nation-states and maybe the focus should shift to building strong, collaborative regions within a united Afrika instead. To succeed in either of these efforts, political systems need to be more flexible and tolerant in order to achieve the following:

1. A greater degree of ownership by local village communities of the public political space.

2. Diluting the practical negative impact created by artificial political boundaries that we inherited from our colonial masters. These man-made boundaries are definitely not what our ancestors and God had in mind. They are too artificial, impractical, divide rather than unite Afrikans, and no wonder, all the regional institutions that we try to build, such as the Afrikan Union, SADC, East-Afrika Community, ECOWAS, as well as good concepts such as NEPAD, find it difficult to express themselves legitimately in any country or better still, in an ordinary Afrikan village. Until such time that all these ambitious regional and Pan-Afrikan institutions have full meaning and ownership at village level in Afrika, they will simply serve the unfortunate role of delaying, rather than accelerating the Afrikan Renaissance.

3. I have just one last point to make on this issue of politics and governance and that is to say that the traditional forms of leadership that we have in Afrika are just as legitimate as any other forms of leadership within their context. I am saying this because there is a lot of confusion in Afrika today as to what constitutes legitimate leadership.

In general one observes that the pre-occupation with multiparty politics and general elections in Afrika has diverted the attention of Afrikan people away from people being governed, and back to the instruments of the nation state. There is abundant evidence today that, merely having legitimate political elections in a country, is still a far cry from actually establishing a democratic nation-state. Once again, this is similar to building a house starting from the roof to the foundation. Democracy in Afrika can only be achieved bottom-up, through participatory village-level processes.

It is important for Afrikans to recognise that different types of situations require different types of leadership systems and that elections are not the only legitimate way to leadership. For instance, *appointed* leadership is legitimate in situations where the appointee is simply discharging a delegated responsibility by a higher authority. *Selected* leadership is most legitimate where certain skills, knowledge and experience are required to be able to execute the responsibilities. In this case it is best to select from the best that you have in the community or in the situation. *Inherited* leadership is most legitimate where there is strong belief in the community that the departed leaders are the rightful owners of the area or community and therefore only their descendants can keep the connection between the present, the past and the future. There is also *rotational,* traditional leadership, which is practiced through the existence of a number of recognised families and or extended families, who all have a right to leadership positions on a rotational basis in the community.

Legitimacy of leadership is therefore a function of relevance and acceptability within a culture and or situation, rather than a function of a process such as elections. This is important for Afrikan governments to remember as we spearhead the Renaissance, because all these legitimate forms of leadership, including the traditional, have to be supported, strengthened and modernised, so that they stay current and relevant to today's leadership needs at all levels.

Most governments have constitutions and systems that throw sufficient doubt on the legitimacy of traditional leadership institutions. To make matters worse, some governments and political parties take advantage of this situation, by further exploiting traditional institutions for narrow, short-term political gain. In general, Afrikan governments, emulating their colonial masters, are not really interested in the system of traditional leadership itself, they focus their attention on individual leaders such as Chiefs and Village Heads and use those individual offices to peddle their political agenda, whilst investing nothing, or very little, in promoting the consultative and participatory democracy principles of the traditional leadership system. You will notice that in most countries traditional leaders are virtually co-opted into the civil service, with some kind of a nominal representation at national level in Parliament or other such bodies. Quite often they end up with salaries or perks to go with their title. This development pulls traditional leaders away from their traditional system, so that instead of playing the traditional role, they start behaving like 'executive' leaders. In reality, traditional Leadership in Afrika is not about ruling, or holding executive power. This means that the consultative political system is more important than the positions of Chief and other traditional leadership positions. It is important therefore to recognise that an Afrikan Renaissance is unlikely if rebuilding a community is based on focus on Chiefs and those in position, rather than rebuilding the entire consultative and collective action-leadership system.

In all Afrikan countries today we also have modern-day communities either far-removed from traditional formation or communities that simply do not function through traditional leadership. This would include, for example, urban and peri-urban areas and informal settlements of displaced people. In this situation the most legitimate forms of leadership are likely to be a combination of elected and or selected leaders. In this case it is still important for such leadership to discharge their responsibilities based on the consultative consensus-building and collective action-leadership principles that we have in traditional systems.

5. Economics and Business

The 'General Theory' predicts that the following paradigm shift in terms of economics and business theory and practice is necessary in order to shape the right policy environment for greater economic prosperity accompanying the Afrikan Renaissance:

The first important principle is that family businesses and family farms are the most effective and efficient means of building the local and national economy. There is overwhelming evidence already existing from various Afrikan countries that small family businesses and farms best conform with Afrikan circumstances.

Economic policy therefore, including the building of economic and financial institutions, requires governments to respond to and give priority to those institutions that are most relevant and capable of supporting small and particularly rural family businesses.

Secondly, we have to build a strong rural economy before we can have a great national economy. This is because in Afrika most of our people are living in rural areas. In addition, because poverty is concentrated in rural areas, it follows that we need to address this problem right there, before we assume wrongly that urban centres are capable of creating sufficient jobs to employ all these migrating rural people.

In order to speed up the growth of the modern part of the economy in terms of urban industrial manufacturing sectors, it is still important for us to ensure first that our rural communities are capable of producing abundant food at a low cost, as a pre-requisite for an efficient, urban-based labour economy. In other words, urban workers need low-cost food available in abundance, before we can fully industrialise the economy. And that food has to be produced by small rural producers on family farms.

Sadly, today most urban centres in Afrika are flooded with rural migrants who are prematurely trying to escape rural poverty, ending up in urban centres where none of our big cities have sufficient jobs or infrastructure to accommodate them.

Further still, we have to learn from our Asian counterparts, who have done a much better job of investing in their rural people and rural communities, improving basic social services such as education, health, as well as economic infrastructure such as roads, feeder roads, water reticulation, electrification and so on. This in itself promotes the rural economy and allows rural peoples to acquire sophisticated social and business skills, before they try to migrate to urban areas.

Another important principle is that the economic revitalisation of rural communities has to be based on improving their capacity to add value to products and services at village level. On the basis of *Unhu-Ubuntu-Botho* principles, business is about relationships. Wealth creation therefore is a direct result of adding value at home and exchanging the goods and services locally with relatives, neighbours and friends. This is the only way to add value to rural society, otherwise what we see currently happening is rural people continuing to try and produce raw materials at higher and higher cost and less and less value for themselves. In general, exporting goods longer distances to urban markets has fuelled poverty in rural areas and accelerated the premature migration of the rural poor to urban poor.

The economic principle is to add value and circulate the wealth within your family and community first before 'exporting' to other communities and urban areas..

Then lastly, there is the Machobane principle, which I am borrowing from the great Afrikan warrior of the Kingdom of Lesotho, Mr Machobane. The Machobane principle is that Afrikans should first try and work for themselves, rather than being employed by somebody else. Most of the important qualities necessary for a growing economy are to be found in independent-thinking business entrepreneurs at all levels. This is particularly important in order to rebuild the rural economic capabilities

Before I dwell on Mr Machobane's ideas, let me first explain some basic concepts around poverty in Afrika. Most poverty at community level today is physical poverty that is experienced mostly through Afrikans relying more and more on things they do not produce and at the same time producing more and more things they don't rely on. By doing this, we are eroding our asset base, both physically and biologically in the form of trees and rivers.

All this is compounded by the growing intellectual poverty, I have already discussed, in the sense that we Afrikans do not value or leverage our own knowledge to best advantage.

So the wealth-creating strategies at community level include firstly, an asset-based community development strategy, which means building physical and biological assets more aggressively than in the past. Rural communities have to build their own wells for water, small dams, roads, feeder roads in terms of physical capital. In addition, we need to aggressively grow greater biological capital in the form of planting more trees, herbs for medicines and generally improving the genetic quality of these natural products.

I have already expressed the need to add value and circulate these products within the community as a means of not only growing wealth, but making the wealth work for communities.

The third principle is where the Machobane principle comes in. And this principle is simple: *refuse to be a dog*. According to Machobane, if you are employed by somebody else, you are a dog. Why? Because you are totally reliant on the master for your food and maintenance. Even if the master kicks the dog, the dog may go howling away into the bush for a little way, but certainly will return back to the master as soon as possible, knowing fully well that it cannot survive without the master. The basic message is: start your own business or start your own projects. Do not work for somebody else, particularly after a certain age.

The fourth point is, be sure to bequeath to your children all the life and survival skills you have acquired in your own lifetime. And these skills have to be broad to include food production and preservation, home improvement, as well as managing family projects and management of money and other financial resources.

Fifthly, we have to learn to transmute problems and challenges into business opportunities. So, instead of feeling sorry for ourselves in the face of trouble, we should embrace some of these as real opportunity for producing a new good or providing a new service, around the challenge.

In addition, we can also produce considerable business value from our culture and traditions and combined with a cottage-industry approach to produce various products such as functional art, crafts, as well as other home-improvement products and fashion, rural family businesses have a lot of great opportunity for lucrative, high-value businesses in the future.

Finally, the real economic value that is still untapped in the rural Afrika resides in the natural resource assets, in particular land, water and trees, as well as other plants. The tragedy is that these assets are hardly translated into real wealth for the rural poor families. Moreover, the real legal ownership of these assets has, once again, shifted hands over the colonial and pre-colonial period, from local ownership to state ownership. This basically means that most rural Afrikans have no real legal ownership of the land they reside on and use on a daily basis.

As part of the Commission of Inquiry into Land Tenure Systems in Zimbabwe that I headed and that I referred to earlier, I was astounded to find that rural Afrikans have been systematically disenfranchised of their historical ownership of all these resources that are practically their possessions. In essence, all these assets are equivalent to 'latent' capital, which has not been mobilised to contribute to the wealth of the community. It is my strong belief that as part of the Afrikan Renaissance all Afrikan governments have to re-examine their national constitutions and legal framework around land issues and start commissioning and mobilising mass reforms which would allow all land in a country to have similar economic potential.

In the case of traditional land that was historically held under traditional tenure systems, my work and other people's scholarly work in the recent past has demonstrated that traditional land tenure systems embody within themselves all the key ingredients of a modern and secure tenure system. What is missing, therefore, is a legal framework that confers back to the traditional leadership system, the administrative role to confer the various land-rights usually accorded to commercial land.

The basket of four tenure rights that need to be recognised and secured in the traditional system as it used to be, traditionally, include the rights to use the land, the rights to transfer the land, the rights to exclude and or include others, such as your children in using the land and finally, the right of having enforcement in place by the traditional system and or government in securing those rights against abuse by others. By conferring the traditional system administrative function over these rights, it is therefore possible for the family and the village *Dare*, to confer leases, title deeds and other Western-style instruments that allow latent capital to come to life. It is important to recognise that in most Afrikan tenure systems, traditionally held land is allocated to family and not individuals. However, this should not present any challenges in 'enlivening' land as capital, as long as the family structures are fully consulted in any transaction with land and other assets.

The land tenure issue therefore is bigger than its economic significance. Land tenure in rural Afrika represents the most significant system of self-governance at local level. This means that resolving the land tenure issue is part and parcel of establishing the *Unhu-Ubuntu-Botho* ethos of local participatory democracy.

Conclusion

I know that the central message in this book can be regarded and will be and should be regarded by most Afrikans as common sense. I am thankful that you have taken time to go through this book. The fact that you've read the book to the end suggests to me that I am probably preaching to the converted. After all, most Afrikans instinctively understand these issues that I've been trying to explain. The challenge therefore is not in finding people who believe in these ideas, the real challenge is at the individual level: the challenge is what are you going to do about it?

Given the formidable challenges that Afrika faces today, it is easy to give up and assume that there isn't much one can do as an individual. Part of this book and in conclusion, is to suggest strongly that there is a lot that you can do!

For a start it is important for you to immediately embark on your own journey of self-discovery. In fact, this book should serve just as an appetiser. You should go ahead and map out all the important aspects of

Unhu-Ubuntu-Botho pathways that you commit to exploring for yourself on a daily basis.

So this book is just aiming to help and encourage you to be the change agent that you already are!

And remember: I am, because we are.

Afrikan Language Editions

Afrikan Intelligence in Afrikan Languages

Would you like to read this book in an Afrikan Language?

mandala publishers

is committed to publishing books about Afrikan issues, knowledge and stories in Afrikan languages in order to contribute to a body of knowledge in widely-spoken Afrikan languages and to increase accessibility of this valuable material to all Afrikans.

Visit our website on **www.afrikanintelligence.com** to keep track of which Afrikan language editions of books published by mandala publishers have appeared or are about to appear. Make sure to secure an advance order for limited First Editions, or join the exclusive **Afrikan Book Club**.

Calling all existing or new Afrikan authors:

Were you born in Afrika? Have you published a book that you would like to publish again in an Afrikan language? Or have you written a book that is relevant to Afrika in the 21st Century?

Or are you dreaming of writing a book?

Then write to us today at:

info@itea-afrika.com for more information.

www.afrikanintelligence.com

About the Author
Mandivamba Rukuni

Before joining the W. K. Kellogg Foundation, Rukuni was a
Professor of Agricultural Economics at the University of
Zimbabwe. He was appointed as Chair of the Zimbabwe Land
Commission by President Robert Mugabe to look into the
sensitive issues of land use and land reform in Zimbabwe. He also
has undertaken several assignments for international agencies,
including the United Nations Food and Agriculture Organization,
the World Bank, the U.S. Agency for International Development,
and philanthropies such as the Rockefeller Foundation. He earned
a Diploma in agriculture from Chibero Agriculture College in
Zimbabwe, as well as a Bachelor's Degree in agriculture from the
University of Zimbabwe. He took his Master's Degree in tropical
agricultural development from the University of Reading,
England, and went on to earn his Doctorate in Agricultural
Economics from the University of Zimbabwe.

Communicate with the author at
being.afrikan@gmail.com